# THE FRENCH MARKET

# THE FRENCH MARKET

## More recipes from a French kitchen

## Joanne Harris and Fran Warde

Doubleday

LONDON · TORONTO · SYDNEY · AUCKLAND · JOHANNESBURG

TRANSWORLD PUBLISHERS
61–63 Uxbridge Road, London W5 5SA
a division of The Random House Group Ltd

RANDOM HOUSE AUSTRALIA (PTY) LTD
20 Alfred Street, Milsons Point, Sydney,
New South Wales 2061, Australia

RANDOM HOUSE NEW ZEALAND LTD
18 Poland Road, Glenfield, Auckland 10, New Zealand

RANDOM HOUSE SOUTH AFRICA (PTY) LTD
Endulini, 5a Jubilee Road, Parktown 2193, South Africa

Published 2005 by Doubleday
a division of Transworld Publishers

A catalogue record for this book is available
from the British Library.
ISBN 0385 608233

Photography by Debi Treloar
Styling by Helen Trent
Project managed by Mari Roberts
Designed by Fiona Andreanelli
Index by Hilary Bird

Printed in Italy

1 3 5 7 9 10 8 6 4 2

Papers used by Transworld Publishers are natural, recyclable products
made from wood grown in sustainable forests. The manufacturing processes
conform to the environmental regulations of the country of origin.

# Introduction

Surely one of the joys of visiting any country must be the discovery of that country's food. It's the simplest and most effective way to embrace a culture; languages and customs take time to learn, but the gift of food is both immediate and very personal, and the acceptance (or rejection) of that gift may sometimes determine an entire future relationship with the country, its people and its traditions.

My great-grandmother had a particularly simple way of judging character. Supremely unmoved by such things as status, beauty, wealth or influence, she would base her first impression of any guest on one thing – how they behaved at table. If they ate well, they were invited a second time. If not, we never saw them again. Her motto was *Who eats well, lives well*, and it's astonishing how often her judgement proved correct.

My great-grandmother's recipes were such favourites with our family that I included a number of them in *The French Kitchen* – so many, in fact, that when Fran and I began to plan our second cookbook, we realized that I had run out of recipes from my own family. Fortunately, every family, like every region, has its particular traditions, and for this new project Fran and I decided to head for the south-west of France and to take what inspiration we could from families, communities and markets there.

It's a region I have learned to know very well. My grandfather had friends in Nérac, on the river Baïse, and from my first visit I was enchanted by the little town with its crooked half-timbered buildings, its old tanneries and cobbled squares, and the multitude of little flat-bottomed boats that drifted downriver. I welcomed this opportunity to discover it further, and the recipes in this book come to us from the wine-makers, farmers and many other locals who threw themselves so wholeheartedly into this project with us.

There is a saying here that goes: *Fishermen and Gascons are born to lie.* That seems appropriate in Nérac, where *gasconnades* abound (those exuberantly tall tales in which the region specializes), and, if you believe what you hear, every fisherman is descended from a king (or at least a prince) in exile.

There is some reason to believe it; Henri IV lived in Nérac as a young man, and the tales of his many seductions are widespread around the region. Catherine de Médicis and Marguerite de Valois were frequent visitors. Even Shakespeare stayed here for a time, and is said to have written *Love's Labour's Lost* in the Garenne, Henri IV's royal park. Alexandre Dumas, creator of d'Artagnan, the most

famous Gascon of all, lived close by and, passionate gourmet that he was, wrote his *Grand Dictionnaire de Cuisine* just a few miles away. As a fellow-author of both novels and cookery books I feel a particular kinship with Dumas – now there was a man who really enjoyed the various pleasures life had to offer. His writing reflects this, and the inhabitants of the region are proud to claim him as one of their adopted sons.

It's certainly true that this little stretch of the river Baïse is a place where recipes, stories, myths and lies are equally celebrated. The river brings them, like flotsam, and the fertile soil helps them grow. One of these stories became a book called *Chocolat*, which in turn began a chain of other stories, which in turn led Fran and me back here.

Today, I am delighted to see how little has altered. Cafés, shops, streets – even the *chocolaterie*, La Cigale, where Monsieur and Madame Sarrauste have made their own chocolates for over thirty years – all seem quite unchanged. There is some tourism, but not an excessive amount; even the riverboats are still as I remember them, with their groups of colourful – and sometimes unwelcome – travellers. Most of all I remember the markets. Along the Baïse there is a market every day: flower markets, fruit and vegetable markets, and specialist markets dedicated to geese and

ducks, foie gras, Armagnac or honey. Children are especially welcome; as a small child I frequently spent my mornings at one market or another, sampling the various delicacies available. If I had wanted, I could easily have lived for an entire holiday on nothing more than these gifts of fruit, bread, cake and cheese, so generously handed out to *la petite Anglaise*. Of course, to any trader, the pulling power of a small girl by their market stall, enthusiastically eating melon, cake, peaches or plums, has to be worth any number of free samples.

It is from the markets of this region that Fran and I have taken our main inspiration for this cookbook. The market lies at the heart of any rural community. It is a meeting place, an exchange of gossip, an excuse for celebration, for music, for wine-tasting and for the telling of stories. Here, contacts are made, recipes exchanged, extravagant flirtations conducted. Our plan was to scour the markets of the Baïse and its neighbouring regions and to collect ideas, recipes, specialities – and, of course, stories – wherever we went.

It wasn't difficult. The markets of France are a chef's dream: an intoxicating display of seasonal produce, dazzling colours, savoury scents. Everyone is in

competition: the cheese vendor, selling air-dried goat's cheeses rolled in herbs or creamy ewe's cheese flavoured with fennel. The sellers of dried meats: saucisson with blackcurrant, garlic or mushrooms; strong cured ham; strings of peppery salami. Everything is so tempting; the stalls selling brioche, honey and the little sweets called *Amours de Fleurette* (there's a story there, too, of a local girl seduced by a young prince, whose tragic death is still commemorated in sugar and chocolate). Here, fruit and vegetables still depend upon the seasons; a festival celebrates the first cherries, the new asparagus, the autumn mushrooms. In England, it's all too easy to forget the seasons – to be lured by the promise of out-of-season strawberries or watery tomatoes or floury-tasting apples with little to recommend them but regularity of shape.

Here, the wares are anything but regular. Huge, misshapen Marmande tomatoes; giant purple aubergines; striped melons; fat, golden-skinned kiwis; raspberries so ripe that they almost disintegrate to the touch. Most farmers use the traditional methods; many openly flout regulations by selling non-standard, unapproved varieties of fruit and vegetables. Cheeses are defiantly unpasteurized; geese and ducks are reared by hand; cash crops imposed two or three decades ago are gradually being replaced by truffle oaks, fruit trees and rediscovered varieties of potato.

This return to tradition has caused some friction between the locals and the officials from Brussels. One bee-keeper, a man of seventy, told me the sad story of how the authorities had used EU regulations to ban him from selling the traditionally produced honey that has been his family's livelihood for three generations.

*How do you manage?* I asked him.

*Oh, I sell postcards now. Five euros each.*

*Five euros? Isn't that a bit steep for just one postcard?*

*Perhaps*, he said, with a gleam in his eye. *But each one comes with a free pot of honey.*

It is this Gascon spirit of enjoyment, tradition and enterprise that Fran and I have tried to recapture in *The French Market*. Most of the recipes are simple; all are based on the idea that with good seasonal ingredients to hand, no chef can go far wrong; and all are designed to be tried, tested, adapted and recreated to suit you, your kitchen and the company you keep.

# Soups & Savouries

Soups are a wonderful way of using the many and varied seasonal vegetables that are one of the principal joys of the French market. Pumpkins, mushrooms, chestnuts and squash in autumn; broad beans, sweet green peas and watercress in summer; sweet potatoes, haricot beans, celeriac and carrots throughout the winter. Some of these soups are designed to form the basis of an entire meal, while others serve to stimulate the palate in readiness for the main course. In both cases, they are all delicious, simple and extremely satisfying to make.

The better the stock, the tastier the soup, so make your own if you can. For home-made stock, take bones or carcass from beef, chicken or lamb (do not mix), place in a large pan, cover with water and add onion, garlic, carrot, leek, bay leaf, thyme, salt and pepper. Bring to the boil, simmer gently for 1½ hours, strain and leave to cool. Skim off any fat that floats to the surface and use as required.

The light dishes that follow the soups are ideal with crudités for quick, simple summer dishes, or could be served as individual small courses as part of a more substantial celebration meal.

POTIRON

du Jardin de Mère
7 80

## SOUPE PRINTANIÈRE

*This fresh, creamy green soup is a terrific way to celebrate the arrival of summer's first broad beans, so tender they can even be eaten raw.*

Preparation: 30 minutes
Cooking: 45 minutes

Serves 6

2 tbsp olive oil
3 onions, finely chopped
100g bacon, diced
2 cloves of garlic, crushed, peeled and
 chopped
1.2 litres chicken or vegetable stock
1.5kg broad beans, shelled (or 500g
 excluding pods)
sea salt
freshly ground black pepper
fresh flat-leaf parsley, chopped, to serve

Heat the oil in a large pan. Add the onion and bacon and brown for 5 minutes. Add the garlic and cook for a further 2 minutes, then pour in the stock and add about three-quarters of the shelled beans. Bring to the boil and simmer gently for 30 minutes. Blend until smooth. Add the remaining broad beans and simmer for a further 5 minutes. Season with salt, pepper and parsley, mix well and serve.

## SOUPE AU CHOU-FLEUR

*This luscious, creamy white soup is best made with the freshest, youngest cauliflowers of the season. The tender slices of Brie melt into the soup to make an even more luxurious consistency.*

Preparation: 15 minutes
Cooking: 25 minutes

Serves 6

25g butter
2 shallots, diced
3 sticks of celery, diced
1 large cauliflower, trimmed and
 cut into florets
1 tsp Dijon mustard
2 bay leaves
3 sprigs of thyme
1.2 litres chicken or vegetable stock
sea salt
freshly ground black pepper
freshly grated nutmeg
200ml single cream
100g Brie and chopped chives,
 to serve

Place the butter, shallots and celery in a saucepan and fry gently for 5 minutes without browning. Add the cauliflower florets, mustard, bay leaves, thyme and stock. Bring to the boil and simmer for 20 minutes. Remove the bay leaves and thyme sprigs, and blend until smooth. Season with salt, pepper and nutmeg, and stir in the cream. Garnish with slices of Brie and chopped chives, and serve.

# SOUPE AUX MOULES

*This thick, rich soup of mussels, saffron, wine and cream works especially well with chilli garlic bread, which is Anouchka's favourite, or thick slices of pain poilâne. I also like to serve the soup with most of the mussels in their shells; I think that one of the pleasures of eating mussels is the time that it takes, and the voluptuous sensation of eating with your fingers. Try it both ways, and see which you like best.*

Preparation: 20 minutes
Cooking: 30 minutes

Serves 6

3 tbsp olive oil
3 shallots, chopped
2 cloves of garlic, crushed, peeled and
    chopped
50g flour
500ml fish stock
generous pinch of saffron
100ml double cream
sea salt
freshly ground black pepper
200ml white wine
2kg mussels (shelled weight 600g)
bunch of flat-leaf parsley, chopped

Heat the oil and fry the shallots gently for 4 minutes, then add the garlic and cook for a further minute. Sprinkle in the flour and stir well to absorb all the oil. Slowly add the stock, mixing to make a smooth broth. Add the saffron, cream and seasoning and simmer for 15 minutes. In another large pan heat the wine. Add all the mussels, then cover and cook for 6 minutes until they are all open. Discard any that are not open by this stage.

Drain the mussels, reserving the liquid. Strain the liquid and add to the soup. Allow the mussels to cool, then remove the meat from the shells and add to the soup. Simmer for 2 minutes. Add the parsley and serve.

## SOUPE AUX HARICOTS

*Fran likes to use cannellini beans for this recipe, although white haricot beans (which are similar in taste, though a little smaller) will do just as well. Choose the tastiest tomatoes you can find – this dish is an excellent way to use those enormous, misshapen Marmande tomatoes you see on French market stalls.*

Preparation: 30 minutes, plus overnight
   soaking
Cooking: 2½ hours

Serves 6

300g dried cannellini or white haricot
   beans, soaked overnight, drained
2 tbsp olive oil
2 onions, chopped
2 cloves of garlic, crushed, peeled and
   chopped
1.2 litres chicken stock
400g uncooked ham, chopped
800g tomatoes
2 bay leaves
3 sprigs of thyme
sea salt
freshly ground black pepper
bunch of flat-leaf parsley, chopped

Soak the beans overnight in plenty of cold water. Drain and rinse them and place in a large pan with the olive oil, onions, garlic and stock. Add the chopped ham, bring to the boil and simmer gently.

   Peel the tomatoes by making a small cross in the skin and plunging them into boiling water for 20 seconds. Remove and peel the skins off. Chop the tomatoes roughly and add to the soup, along with the bay leaves and thyme, then simmer for 1½ hours. Season to taste, remove the bay leaves and thyme sprigs, add plenty of parsley, and serve.

# POTAGE BONNE FEMME

*The 'bonne femme' in this case is Madame Labadie of Nérac, who grows the biggest and best leeks in the entire region. Fran has slightly adapted her family recipe, but if you want to be entirely authentic, substitute two Vache Qui Rit cheese triangles for the fromage frais. Madame Labadie has been making soup this way since the war, she tells me, and completely disapproves of such frivolities as fromage frais. However, in an emergency, and with no Vache Qui Rit to hand, she concedes that fromage frais might do almost as well …*

Preparation: 30 minutes
Cooking: 1 hour

Serves 6

25g butter
500g leeks, cut into matchsticks
600g potatoes, diced
20g plain flour
1 litre chicken or vegetable stock
sea salt
freshly ground black pepper
2 tbsp fromage frais
chopped fresh herbs – chives, flat-leaf
    parsley – to serve

Melt the butter in a pan, add the leeks and potatoes and fry gently for a few minutes without browning. Sprinkle in the flour and mix well to absorb the butter. Slowly add the stock, stirring well, then season, bring to the boil, reduce the heat and simmer gently for 20 minutes. Blend if you prefer a smooth consistency, then add the fromage frais and herbs, and serve.

## SOUPE DU VIGNERON

*This lovely autumn recipe is typical of the south-west, and combines the season's first wild mushrooms with the region's favourite speciality – wine. Use white wine for a lighter, sweeter taste, and red for a richer, darker flavour.*

Preparation: 20 minutes
Cooking: 1¼ hours

Serves 6

700g onions
50g butter
4 tbsp olive oil
250g wild or chestnut mushrooms
3 cloves of garlic, crushed, peeled and
    chopped
750ml chicken or vegetable stock
500ml red or white wine
herbs: 2 bay leaves, 3 sprigs of thyme
sea salt
freshly ground black pepper
6 slices stale bread, cut into cubes

Slice the onions as finely as possible. Heat the butter and olive oil in a large pan, add the onions and cook gently until soft and golden, stirring frequently. Add the mushrooms and garlic and cook for a further 10 minutes. Add the stock, wine and herbs, then season to taste with salt and black pepper, bring to the boil and simmer for 45 minutes. This dish is traditionally served with stale bread, which is placed in the bottom of each soup bowl before serving.

# GARBURE

*This is a very old winter soup recipe from the south-west of France. Everyone has a slightly different version of it, but it should always be rich, thick, tasty and satisfying. It is one of those dishes that is best reheated, so if you can't resist eating it all straight away, make double.*

Preparation: 20 minutes, plus overnight
  soaking
Cooking: 2 hours

Serves 6

300g haricot beans
500g uncooked ham or bacon, chopped
1.2 litres water
1 bouquet garni (bay, thyme, parsley, sage,
  marjoram)
2 onions, chopped
2 cloves of garlic, crushed, peeled and
  chopped
350g potatoes, chopped
200g green or white cabbage, chopped
2 tbsp confit d'oie
200g shelled broad beans
sea salt
freshly ground black pepper
6 slices brown rustic bread
300g Roquefort

Soak the beans overnight in plenty of cold water. Drain and rinse them, place in a large saucepan with the ham or bacon, water, bouquet garni, onions and garlic, cover, bring to the boil and simmer for an hour and a half. Add the chopped potatoes, cabbage, confit d'oie and broad beans and simmer for a further 45 minutes. Season to taste – although sometimes the cured ham or bacon has enough natural salt in it, so check before you add any. Cut the bread into cubes and place in the soup bowls. Crumble the Roquefort over the bread, then ladle in the soup and serve.

# GOUGÈRE AU JAMBON

*The traditional gougère is made as a single large ring, although you could also make it as a number of little choux pastry puffs. Either way, gougère is simple to make, and works wonderfully with a simple green salad or as an apéritif with a glass of wine or floc. For simplicity's sake, I have made this gougère in an ovenproof dish that roughly shapes the choux pastry and makes a wonderfully easy and tasty supper dish.*

Preparation: 40 minutes
Cooking: 60 minutes

Serves 6

**For the choux pastry:**
210ml water
75g butter
100g plain flour
3 medium eggs, beaten
75g Beaufort cheese, grated

**For the ham filling:**
2 tbsp olive oil
25g butter
2 shallots, chopped
2 cloves of garlic, crushed, peeled and chopped
30g plain flour
150ml ham or chicken stock
75ml dry white wine
freshly ground black pepper
2 tsp seed mustard
450g cooked ham, roughly chopped

Heat the oven to 200°C/gas 6. Grease a 20cm by 25cm shallow ovenproof dish.

To make the pastry, place the water and butter in a medium saucepan and bring to the boil. Remove from the heat and stir until all the butter has melted. Add the flour and rapidly beat until the mixture is smooth, then return to the heat and beat constantly until the mixture falls away from the side of the pan. Remove from the heat and allow to cool for 5 minutes. Add a little beaten egg and mix well. Repeat until the mixture has reached a dropping consistency. Now add half of the grated cheese and mix. Spoon the choux pastry mix around the edge of the prepared dish, place in the oven and bake for 30 minutes.

For the filling, heat the olive oil and butter in a pan. Add the shallots, fry for 3 minutes, then add the garlic and cook for a further minute. Remove the pan from the heat and mix in the flour, making a roux. Return to a low heat, add a little stock and mix until smooth. Repeat until all the stock is incorporated. Add the wine, pepper and mustard. Mix well, bringing to the boil for 10 seconds, stirring constantly so that the sauce does not stick to the bottom of the pan. Add the ham, then spoon the mixture into the dish and sprinkle the remaining cheese on top. Reduce the heat to 150°C/gas 2, return the dish to the oven and bake for a further 25 minutes until bubbling and golden.

# FEUILLETÉ AU FROMAGE

*This dish combines the typical inland flavours of thyme, bacon and regional cheeses with a light and flaky pastry base. Don't stress too much over the puff pastry; if you don't have time to make your own, the ready-made stuff works just as well …*

Preparation: 40 minutes , plus 1½ hours' pastry resting
Cooking: 1 hour 15 minutes

Serves 6

*For the puff pastry (pâte feuilletée):*
250g plain flour
pinch of salt
100–150ml ice-cold water
1 tsp lemon juice
250g butter, at room temperature
1 beaten egg, for brushing

*For the filling:*
1kg red onions
2 tbsp olive oil
100ml white wine
200g lardons (optional)
3 sprigs of thyme
100g Port Salut or Chaumes cheese
sea salt
freshly ground black pepper

To make the pastry, sift the flour and salt into a bowl. Make a well in the middle. Add the water and lemon juice and mix together, kneading quickly to a smooth dough. Wrap in cling film and allow to rest for 30 minutes. Meanwhile, place the block of butter between two large sheets of greaseproof paper or cling film and, using a rolling pin, flatten it out until it measures about 20 by 15cm, then return it to the fridge. On a lightly dusted surface roll out the pastry to about 25 by 45cm. Place the flattened butter in the middle of the pastry and fold the two ends in to cover the butter. Turn by 90 degrees and roll out to 25 by 45cm again. Then repeat: fold one third up and then the remaining third, turn by 90 degrees and roll out again. Wrap and place in the fridge to cool and rest for 30 minutes. Repeat the above process twice, and rest the pastry for 30 minutes before rolling it into the required shape.

Slice the onions very finely (using a mandolin if you have one). Heat the oil and add the onions. Fry briskly for 5 minutes, then add the wine, lardons and 2 sprigs of thyme. Reduce the heat and cook for 30 minutes, stirring frequently until the liquid evaporates.

Heat the oven to 220°C/gas 7. Roll out the pastry into a rectangle about 21cm by 30cm. Place on a greased baking sheet, mark all over with a fork and work the edges with a fine-bladed knife (see overleaf). Place in the oven and bake for 12 minutes. Remove and cover with the cooked onions. Slice the cheese finely and layer over the top of the onions, season and scatter the leaves from the remaining sprig of thyme over. Brush the exposed pastry with egg and place in the oven for 15 minutes. Reduce the heat to 160°C/gas 3 and cook for a further 15 minutes.

## TARTELETTES AUX CHAMPIGNONS DES BOIS

*There are so many different kinds of mushroom available at different times of year that you can afford to be creative with this recipe, although it's always best to choose whatever is fresh and in season. Chanterelles have a subtle apricot scent; cèpes a rich, almost meaty taste, and the wonderfully named trompettes de la mort have a strong, wild flavour that works very well in this tasty, colourful autumn dish.*

Preparation: 40 minutes , plus 1½ hours' pastry resting
Cooking: 20 minutes

Serves 6

*For the puff pastry (pâte feuilletée):*
250g plain flour
pinch of salt
100–150ml ice-cold water
1 tsp lemon juice
250g butter, at room temperature
1 beaten egg, for brushing

*For the mushroom filling:*
60g butter
3 shallots, very finely chopped
3 cloves of garlic, crushed, peeled and chopped
700g wild mushrooms
50ml white wine
4 tbsp double cream
sea salt
freshly ground black pepper
chopped fresh flat-leaf parsley

Prepare the puff pastry using the previous recipe (unless you're using the ready-made variety) and return it to the fridge.

Heat the oven to 220°C/gas 7. Roll out the pastry to 30cm by 40cm and cut into 6 equal-sized pieces. Using a fork, make indentations all over the base (this helps to keep the pastry flat when cooking). Cut a 5mm strip from around the edge of each piece, brush the edges with beaten egg and lay the thin strips back on the pastry base, like a picture frame. Work the edge of the pastry by gently marking each edge with horizontal indentations using a fine-bladed knife; this helps the pastry to rise and form a neat edge. Place on a baking sheet, put it into the oven and cook for 12–15 minutes until golden. Remove from the oven and reduce the heat to 180°C/gas 4.

Melt the butter in a large pan, add the shallots and fry gently for 5 minutes without browning. Add the garlic and mushrooms and fry for a further 4 minutes, stirring frequently. Return the pastry cases to the oven for 4 minutes. Add the wine and cream to the mushrooms, increase the heat and simmer for 1 minute. Season and add the parsley. Spoon into the cooked pastry cases and serve at once.

# BRIOCHE AUX CHAMPIGNONS

*This recipe calls for the largest and tastiest mushrooms you can find. As an alternative to the mushrooms listed below, or for a change, try the incomparable cèpe, which by itself tastes good enough to turn the most committed carnivore into a vegetarian…*

Preparation: 15 minutes
Cooking: 15 minutes

Serves 6

3 tbsp olive oil
50g butter
6 large flat mushrooms
200g girolles
2 cloves of garlic, crushed, peeled and
  chopped
100ml white wine
3 tbsp double cream
sea salt
freshly ground black pepper
6 slices of brioche
chopped chives, to serve

Heat the olive oil and butter in a large pan. Add the flat mushrooms and cook at a medium heat for 8 minutes, turning occasionally. Add the girolles and fry for a further 3 minutes, then add the garlic and cook for 1 minute. Increase the heat; add the wine, double cream and seasoning, and toss well until the liquid evaporates and the mixture thickens.

Toast the brioche and serve with the mushroom mixture, sprinkled with chopped chives.

# TARTE AU CHÈVRE

*A goat's cheese tart makes a lovely summer dish,*
*served with a crisp green salad or a handful of*
*peppery pink radishes, and although Fran will*
*probably kill me for saying so, I see no shame in*
*using ready-made pastry if that preparation time*
*seems rather excessive …*

Preparation: 30 minutes, plus an hour's chilling
Cooking: 1½ hours

Serves 6

*For the pastry (pâte à foncer):*
240g plain flour
pinch of salt
60g butter, diced
60g lard or vegetable fat, diced
2–3 tbsp cold water

*For the filling:*
50g butter
400g leeks, finely sliced
2 eggs
150ml single cream
sea salt
freshly ground black pepper
150g goat's cheese

To make the pastry, place the flour, salt and fat in a bowl and rub together with your fingertips until the texture resembles fine breadcrumbs. Add the water and mix together with a round-bladed knife until the mixture forms a ball. Place on a lightly floured surface and knead lightly until the pastry is evenly blended. Wrap in cling film and place in the fridge to chill for 30 minutes.

Lightly butter a 24cm flan tin. Roll out the pastry on a flour-dusted surface until just larger than the tin. Carefully roll the pastry around the rolling pin and unroll onto the flan tin. Press into the tin and trim any excess with a small knife, then place in the fridge to chill for a further 30 minutes.

Heat the oven to 180°C/gas 4. Line the pastry with baking paper and cooking beans, then place in the oven to cook for 30 minutes. Remove the baking paper and beans and cook for a further 10 minutes.

Melt the butter in a pan. Add the leeks and sweat them for 15 minutes. Beat the eggs, cream and seasoning together in a bowl, add the leeks, mix and pour into the pastry case. Crumble the goat's cheese over the top and bake for 45 minutes.

CHÊVRERi

# CHÈVRE CHAUD À LA GASCONNE

*This recipe is a nicely regional version of the classic warm goat's cheese salad, and provides a splendid opportunity to experiment with the wide variety of goat's cheeses available on French markets. As it ages, goat's cheese gains in flavour but loses moisture, so for this recipe use small cheeses that are firm but not too dry. The naughtily named crottins (droppings) are best for this, rolled in ash, black pepper or herbs for extra flavour. Fran likes pitted black olives; I prefer the jewelled, multicoloured varieties that you can buy by the generous scoop on any market south of La Rochelle, gleaming with oil and heady with chillies – but you decide: it's your kitchen, and your choice.*

Preparation: 30 minutes, plus overnight
    marinating
Cooking: 10 minutes

Serves 6

2 cloves of garlic, crushed and peeled
bunch of fresh basil
200ml olive oil
sea salt
freshly ground black pepper
6 goat's cheese crottins
1 baguette
1 head red chicory
1 head white chicory
50g mixed olives

To make a marinade, chop the garlic and basil, then add the olive oil and seasoning. Pour the marinade into a shallow dish and add the cheeses, making sure they are coated evenly. Cover and refrigerate for 24 hours.

Cut the baguette into 12 thick slices and toast. Cut the cheeses in half crosswise, place on a baking sheet and put under a hot grill until golden (about 5 minutes). Divide the leaves of the chicory and the olives between 6 plates. Place 2 toasts with grilled cheese on each plate, then top with the excess marinade.

# SOUFFLÉ AU ROQUEFORT

*Produced only in Roquefort, in the Aveyron, this is one of the oldest (and strongest!) of French cheeses. According to local legend it was discovered by accident, when a young shepherd boy left his lunch of bread and cheese in a cave and forgot it. Returning some weeks later he discovered that the result of his carelessness was a blue-veined dry cheese that people found strangely appetizing … Serve the soufflé with a green salad.*

Preparation: 25 minutes
Cooking: 40 minutes

Serves 6

50g butter
50g plain flour
250ml milk
150g Roquefort, mashed
freshly grated nutmeg
4 eggs, separated

Heat the oven to 190°C/gas 5. Butter a 1.75-litre soufflé dish. Melt the butter in a small saucepan, remove from the heat and add the flour. Mix to a smooth paste. Slowly add a little milk and stir until blended. Repeat until all the milk has been added, then return to the heat, stirring constantly until the sauce thickens. Remove from the heat. Add the Roquefort, nutmeg and egg yolks, and mix. Whisk the egg whites until stiff. Fold in the Roquefort mixture until evenly blended. Pour into the soufflé dish and cook in the centre of the hot oven for 35–40 minutes until risen and golden. Serve at once.

## CITROUILLE AU JAMBON DE BAYONNE

*This simple but striking combination of air-dried ham and sweet, tender pumpkin makes a wonderful autumn dish. Don't discard the pumpkin seeds; just toast them in the oven with some olive oil and rock salt, and add them to a green salad for a satisfying crunch.*

Preparation: 15 minutes
Cooking: 30 minutes

Serves 6

1kg pumpkin
12 thin slices Bayonne ham
olive oil
sea salt
freshly ground black pepper

Heat the oven to 180°C/gas 4.

Cut the pumpkin into 6 wedges. Cut these in half, remove the seeds, and wrap each piece with the Bayonne ham (if you can't get this, Parma or Serrano ham works very well). Place on a roasting tray, drizzle with olive oil and season with sea salt and black pepper. Bake for 30–40 minutes, so that the pumpkin is tender and the ham nicely crispy.

45

# MAISON LE-MEUR PATISSIER

## CONFISEUR GLACIER
## SALON DE THÉ

PAINS

# Salads & Vegetables

Even if you're not a vegetarian, I can't see how you can fail to be seduced by the amazing selection of multicoloured, multi-shaped fruits and vegetables, mushrooms, nuts, leaves and herbs that can be found on markets in France. Huge fresh bunches of leaves and salads; glossy purple aubergines; red, white, yellow, even blue or black potatoes; cherries and apricots sold not by the pound but by the crate. Here, produce is definitely not uniform; many varieties are available that are not known or used in England, and for me it is one of the joys of being in an unfamiliar place to taste, test and experiment with the unusual in all its forms. Many of these dishes can easily serve as main courses or may be prepared as accompaniments to meat or fish, as required.

Salads are one of the most creative and versatile areas of food preparation. This is fast, tasty food at its best, vibrant with colours, textures and flavours – a perfect excuse for an impulse-buy. Hot or cold, anything goes – and for those of you who still associate the salad with iceberg lettuce and dieters' fare, think of fresh goat's cheeses, rolled in herbs and toasted on brioche, served on a bed of peppery rocket with a drizzle of balsamic vinegar, or buttery avocados tossed in lime juice, or peppery pink radishes straight from the garden, or green herbs, heady with sunlight, with sliced foie gras and sweet persimmons fresh from the tree. Salads are a celebration of the best of the French market (where many of the fruit and vegetables have been picked that same morning), and at best should excite the most jaded palate with a perpetual rush of flavours.

Once prepared, salads should never be refrigerated; this kills the taste and perpetuates the 'iceberg lettuce' fallacy that all salads are dull. Dressing, too, is an essential, and for the most part I like to use a simple vinaigrette – three tablespoons of oil, 1 tablespoon of vinegar, 1 teaspoon of mustard and seasoning – although fans of creamy dressings will also find plenty in this chapter to satisfy their taste buds.

## AÏOLI

*This creamy garlic dressing works wonderfully with a variety of dishes, including salads, crudités and most fish dishes.*

Preparation: 20 minutes

Serves 6, with some left over

4 cloves of garlic, crushed, peeled and
   chopped
sea salt
3 egg yolks
1 tbsp white wine vinegar
1 tsp Dijon mustard
400ml olive oil
juice of $\frac{1}{2}$ lemon
freshly ground black pepper

Pound the garlic with the salt using a pestle and mortar until smooth and creamy. Add the egg yolks, vinegar and mustard, and mix to rich creamy consistency. Transfer to a bowl and very slowly add the olive oil, whisking constantly. Add the lemon juice, pepper and blend. If you prefer a thinner consistency, add a spoonful of warm water. The aïoli will keep for up to a week in the fridge.

## MAYONNAISE

*Real mayonnaise is so easy to make, and so much better than the shop-bought variety, that I wonder why anyone buys the bottled stuff at all. Use a light, mild olive oil for a subtle flavour that will not overwhelm the dish, or try using half olive oil to half vegetable oil. Serve with crudités – a selection of raw vegetables, trimmed and cut into slices – for a colourful, simple starter.*

Preparation: 15 minutes

Serves 6, with some left over

3 egg yolks
1 tbsp white wine vinegar
1 tbsp Dijon mustard
400ml olive oil
juice of $\frac{1}{2}$ lemon
freshly ground black pepper

Whisk the egg yolks, vinegar and mustard together to a rich creamy consistency. Very slowly, add the olive oil, whisking constantly until it amalgamates. Add the lemon juice and pepper and blend. If you prefer a thinner consistency, add a spoonful of warm water.

## ROUILLE

*The beauty of this simple mayonnaise-based sauce is its versatility, although it is particularly used to enhance the flavours of salads, fish and fish soup.*

Preparation: 30 minutes

Serves 6, with some left over

4 cloves of garlic, crushed, peeled and
    chopped
1 red chilli, deseeded and chopped
1 red pepper, peeled, deseeded and
    chopped
sea salt
3 egg yolks
1 tbsp white wine vinegar
1 tsp Dijon mustard
400ml olive oil
juice of ½ lemon
freshly ground black pepper

Pound the garlic, chilli and red pepper with the salt in a pestle and mortar until smooth and creamy. Add the egg yolks, vinegar and mustard and mix to a rich creamy consistency. Transfer to a bowl and very slowly add the olive oil, whisking constantly. Add the lemon juice and pepper, and blend. If you prefer a thinner consistency, add a spoonful of warm water.

Try making your own versions by adding any of the following:

Chopped herbs: tarragon, chervil, parsley, basil
Chopped gherkins, capers, shallots, spring onions
Chopped watercress
Curry powder, mango or apricot chutney
Harissa, cumin

## VINAIGRETTE AUX HERBES

*This simple and versatile dressing is great with all vegetables, salads, grilled fish, cold pork and chicken, and can even be added to pasta.*

Preparation: 20 minutes

Serves 6

1 clove of garlic, crushed, peeled and
   chopped
generous bunch of mixed fresh herbs: flat-
   leaf parsley, basil, chives, tarragon
50ml red wine vinegar
1 tsp sugar
2 tsp Dijon mustard
150ml olive oil
sea salt
freshly ground black pepper

Place the chopped garlic in a bowl. Remove the herb leaves from the stalks and chop very finely. Add to the garlic with the vinegar, sugar and mustard. Mix well. Slowly pour in the olive oil, mixing all the time with a whisk or hand-held blender. When all the oil is blended, add seasoning to taste.

## SAUCE AUX NOIX

*This wonderfully rich walnut dressing is excellent with crudités, toasted sourdough bread or as a simple pasta sauce.*

Preparation: 20 minutes

Serves 6

100g shelled walnuts
3 cloves of garlic, crushed, peeled and
   chopped
sea salt
freshly ground black pepper
200ml walnut oil
bunch of flat-leaf parsley, finely chopped

Pound or blend together the walnuts and garlic into a fine paste. Mix in a tablespoon of warm water and season. Slowly whisk in the walnut oil (the sauce will thicken and take on a texture similar to mayonnaise), then mix in the chopped parsley.

## SALADE DE MARMANDE

*Marmande tomatoes are one of the highlights of the summer season, with their firm skins and intense flavour. Their irregular shapes and colours ranging from stripy yellow to pillar-box red may look peculiar, but the taste is phenomenal, and they need nothing but a drizzle of olive oil and a bunch of spicy, locally grown herbs to make a terrific simple meal.*

Preparation: 10 minutes

Serves 6

600g Marmande tomatoes
big bunch of basil or thyme
4 tbsp olive oil
sea salt
freshly ground black pepper

Core the tomatoes and slice them finely. Remove the leaves from the basil stems and chop roughly; strip the thyme leaves off their stalks. Place the tomatoes in a bowl. Add the herbs, olive oil and seasoning. Serve at once with crusty bread.

## SALADE DE CONCOMBRE

*These simple, clean, fresh flavours are perfect for a hot summer's day.*

Preparation: 15 minutes, plus 30 minutes' marinating

Serves 6

2 cucumbers
bunch of dill
juice of 1 lemon
4 tbsp olive oil
sea salt
freshly ground black pepper

Peel the cucumbers and cut in half lengthways. Run a teaspoon down the middle to remove the seeds, then slice finely at an angle and place in a bowl. Chop the dill and add to the bowl along with the lemon juice, olive oil and seasoning, then mix well and leave to marinate for 30 minutes.

## MELON AU FLOC

*'Melons are like men,' my grandmother used to say. 'You have to give them a good feel before you can be sure you've made the right choice.' In this case, it means checking that your melon has a suitably intoxicating scent, is firm to the touch and heavy in the hand. Charentais melons are small, grey-green and stripy, with bright Hallowe'en-pumpkin-coloured flesh and a sweet, musky taste. The stronger the scent, the riper the melon, and a market-ripe melon is usually best eaten on the day of purchase. Slightly unripe melons should be left to ripen, if possible, on an outside window-ledge in the shade. Never refrigerate melons – it kills both taste and scent – but do store them in a cool place. Best with chilled floc (that divine and closely guarded secret of the Gascon region: see page 165), but a decent port will do in an emergency.*

Preparation: 10 minutes

Serves 6

3 Charentais melons
300ml chilled red floc de Gascogne

Cut a small section from the bottom of each melon (making a flat base to set it on). Slice the melons in half through the middle and, with a dessertspoon, scoop out the seeds. Place the prepared melons at the table and fill each hollow with chilled floc.

## SALADE DES CHAMPS DE MER

*This is a salad of gentle flavours: fragrant melon, dill and sea fresh prawns, balanced with a squeeze of lime juice. Fran likes to use peeled prawns for this dish, while I prefer to shell my own.*

Preparation: 10 minutes

Serves 6

2 Charentais melons
500g large prawns, cooked
bunch of dill, chopped
2 tbsp olive oil
$^1/_2$ lemon

Cut a small section from the bottom of each melon (making a flat base to set it on). Slice the melons in half through the middle and, with a dessertspoon, scoop out the seeds. Cut into wedges and either divide between 6 plates or place on one large serving plate, then add the prawns and chopped dill. Drizzle with olive oil and a squeeze of lemon juice.

# SALADE PRINTANIÈRE

*This recipe is so simple that it can only work if made with freshly picked seasonal lettuce and good free-range eggs.*

Preparation: 20 minutes
Cooking: 10 minutes

Serves 6

1 tbsp Dijon mustard
1 small clove of garlic, crushed, peeled and
   chopped
1 tsp sugar
3 tbsp vinegar
8 tbsp olive oil, plus 1 extra for frying
6 eggs
400g smoked lardons, chopped
1 large head of lettuce, washed
sea salt
freshly ground black pepper
bunch of flat-leaf parsley, chopped

Put the mustard, garlic, sugar and vinegar into
a jar and mix well. Add the olive oil, put the lid
on the jar and shake vigorously until blended.

Place the eggs in a pan of warm water, bring
to the boil and simmer for 6 minutes. Drain,
then run cold water into the pan for 2 minutes.

Heat the extra tablespoon of olive oil in a
frying pan. Add the lardons and cook until
nicely crispy. Break the lettuce into a large
bowl; add the seasoning and parsley. Peel the
eggs and cut into quarters, add them to the
salad, and scatter the hot bacon over. Pour over
the vinaigrette, toss, then serve at once.

## POMMES DE TERRE EN SALADE

*This is a terrific way to enjoy the many different varieties of potato that are still available, in gleeful defiance of EU regulations, on markets all over France.*

Preparation: 25 minutes
Cooking: 25 minutes

Serves 6

600g small waxy potatoes
2 tbsp vinegar
1 clove of garlic, crushed, peeled and
   chopped
1 red onion, sliced
300g small tomatoes, sliced
3 tbsp olive oil
sea salt
freshly ground black pepper
bunch of celery leaves, chopped
bunch of chives, chopped
bunch of flat-leaf parsley, chopped

Wash the potatoes and steam for 25 minutes. Slice while still warm and place in a bowl. Add the vinegar, toss and leave to cool for 10 minutes.
   Just before serving, add the garlic, onion, tomatoes, olive oil, seasoning, celery leaves and herbs, and mix well.

## SALADE AUX NOIX

*This salad also works very well with a little dried goat's cheese or Roquefort crumbled into the dressing.*

Preparation: 25 minutes
Cooking: 2 minutes

Serves 6

4 slices of country-style bread
1–2 cloves of garlic, peeled
3 tbsp walnut oil
3 tbsp olive oil
2 tbsp vinegar
1 lettuce, washed
100g walnuts, roughly chopped

Toast the bread and rub on both sides with the garlic. Cut into cubes, place in a bowl, drizzle with 2 tablespoons of the walnut oil and toss. Place the remaining walnut oil in a small bowl and mix with the olive oil and vinegar. Break the lettuce into a large serving bowl, scatter with the garlic toast and walnuts. Add the dressing and serve at once.

## CHÈVRE AUX FIGUES

*For a brief, magical time in midsummer, fresh figs are available in abundance all over France. These have little in common with the limp, anaemic varieties we get in most supermarkets here, but when you can find luscious, firm, ripe black figs it's worth making the most of them. This dish contrasts the musky pink flesh of the summer figs with rich, cured ham and the freshest and most virginal of goat's cheeses.*

Preparation: 30 minutes, plus 30 minutes' chilling

Serves 6

12 ripe figs
12 slices Bayonne ham, or other cured ham
200g young goat's cheese
24 mint leaves, chopped
sea salt
freshly ground black pepper
olive oil

Prepare the figs by removing the stems and then cutting vertically almost to the base. Turn each fig and cut again, squeezing carefully to open it. Chop the ham into 5cm ribbons and place in a bowl. Crumble in the goat's cheese, add the mint leaves and seasoning and mix. Arrange the figs on a large plate and spoon the cheese mixture into the open centre of each fig. Drizzle with olive oil and chill for 30 minutes before serving.

## AVOCAT EN SALADE

*This salad is perfect served slightly warm, on its own or as a sophisticated accompaniment to a simple grilled chicken or fish dish.*

Preparation: 30 minutes
Cooking: 20 minutes

Serves 6

400g purple potatoes, or small waxy variety
2 bunches of chives
1–2 red chillies
bunch of flat-leaf parsley
2 tbsp fromage frais
1 tbsp olive oil
juice of $1/2$ lemon
sea salt
freshly ground black pepper
3 large ripe avocados

Steam the potatoes for 20 minutes, then leave to cool for 10 minutes. Chop the chives, red chillies (with the seeds if you like it spicy) and the leaves from the parsley, and mix together in a bowl. Add the fromage frais, olive oil, lemon juice and seasoning and mix well.

Just before serving, chop the potatoes and place in a serving bowl. Cut the avocados in half, remove the stones and scoop out the flesh with a large spoon. Chop the avocado flesh into pieces, add to the potatoes and mix. Add the dressing and serve.

## SALADE TOULOUSAINE

*This salad can be served hot or cold, but I prefer it just warm, to give the rich flavours a greater intensity.*

Preparation: 25 minutes
Cooking: 30 minutes

Serves 6

4 Toulouse sausages
a little olive oil, for frying
250g chickpeas, prepared
250g haricot beans, prepared
2 tbsp white wine vinegar
4 tbsp olive oil
1 tbsp seed mustard
4 sage leaves, chopped
3 tomatoes, peeled and deseeded
sea salt
freshly ground black pepper

*Note* If you are using tinned chickpeas and haricot beans, look for organic ones as these are better quality. If you are using dried, soak them overnight, drain them, then bring to the boil in a large pan of water. Boil for 10 minutes, reduce the heat and simmer until tender – this takes about 1 to 1½ hours.

Fry the sausages in a little olive oil in a pan for about 15–20 minutes, until golden. Remove and keep warm. Place the chickpeas and haricot beans in the sausage pan, then add the vinegar, olive oil, seed mustard and sage. Cook on a medium heat for 5 minutes, stirring continuously, then remove from the heat. Chop the tomatoes, add to the beans, season, mix well and place in a bowl. Slice the sausages and stir into the salad. Serve hot or cold.

## SALADE TIÈDE AU CAMEMBERT

*This dish relies on contrasting textures for its effect, matching the smoked lardons with spicy young leaves and a luscious Camembert dressing for a really luxurious salad.*

Preparation: 10 minutes
Cooking: 10 minutes

Serves 6

1 tbsp olive oil
200g lardons
250g Camembert
100ml white wine
300g young spinach leaves, washed
300g cooked potatoes, diced
bunch of spring onions
sea salt
freshly ground black pepper

Heat the oil in a frying pan. Add the lardons and cook until crispy. Cut the rind off the Camembert. Place the cheese in a small saucepan with the white wine, and heat very gently. Place the spinach and diced potatoes in a salad bowl, chop the spring onions and add them, along with seasoning. Stir the Camembert and wine together until smooth (do not boil!), then drizzle over the salad and top with the crispy lardons. Serve immediately.

## HARICOTS EN SALADE

*Summer's first broad beans are so young, sweet and delicate that it seems hardly worthwhile making any plans for them at all – we all know that most of them will be eaten straight from the pod long before they see the inside of a cooking pot. This salad makes the most of these tender green beans, just dipped in boiling water and served with a young goat's cheese and the simplest of dressings.*

Preparation: 20 minutes
Cooking: 5 minutes

Serves 6

2kg broad beans in their pods
4 tbsp olive oil
2 tbsp balsamic vinegar
sea salt
freshly ground black pepper
bunch of fresh mint
100g soft goat's cheese

Shell the beans. Bring a large pan of water to the boil, add the beans and simmer for 3 minutes. Drain and refresh in cold water until the beans are cool. Put the beans in a mixing bowl, add the olive oil, balsamic vinegar and seasoning. Remove the mint leaves from the stalks and chop. Add to the beans and toss well. Transfer to a serving bowl, crumble the goat's cheese over the top and serve at once.

## LENTILLES EN SALADE

*Lemon, oil and fresh herbs give a delicate summery flavour to this tomato and lentil salad, delicious on its own or as an excellent accompaniment to grilled fish or chicken.*

Preparation: 25 minutes
Cooking: 20 minutes

Serves 6

300g Puy lentils
6 large tomatoes
2 courgettes
200g sorrel leaves
4 tbsp olive oil
1 clove of garlic, crushed, peeled and
  chopped
sea salt
freshly ground black pepper
juice of 1 lemon

Simmer the lentils in a pan of water for 20 minutes. Peel the tomatoes after plunging them into boiling water for a few seconds. Chop roughly and place in a mixing bowl. Grate the courgettes and shred the sorrel; add to the tomatoes along with the olive oil, garlic, seasoning and lemon juice. Mix well. Drain the lentils, add to the other vegetables, mix well and serve warm or cold.

## SALADE D'AUTOMNE

*Walnuts and home-grown apples give a distinctly autumnal feel to this tasty salad. Perfect for an Indian summer, with chilled rosé.*

Preparation: 30 minutes

Serves 6

1 seasonal lettuce, washed
bunch of chervil, chopped
bunch of flat-leaf parsley, chopped
100g shelled walnuts, roughly chopped
2 Cox's apples
2 tbsp cider vinegar
2 tbsp walnut oil
3 tbsp olive oil
juice of $\frac{1}{2}$ lemon
sea salt
freshly ground black pepper
400g smoked ham, finely sliced

Tear the lettuce into a salad bowl and add the chopped herbs and walnuts. Core and slice the apples and add to the salad. Add the vinegar, walnut oil, olive oil, lemon juice and seasoning and toss well. Gather the finely sliced ham into small bunches and scatter over the top of the salad. Toss lightly and serve.

## CAROTTES RÂPÉES AU MIEL

*This is a delicious way to prepare grated carrots; the result is sweet, spicy and addictive. I'm happy to eat this on its own as a main dish; but it works well with grilled chicken or fish, or as part of a larger selection of salads and cold meats.*

Preparation: 15 minutes

Serves 6

700g carrots
1 tbsp white wine vinegar
3 tbsp runny honey
2 tsp smoked paprika
1 tbsp sesame oil
sea salt
freshly ground black pepper
2 tbsp toasted sesame seeds

Grate the carrots into a bowl. Mix together the vinegar, honey, paprika, sesame oil and seasoning, add to the carrots, and stir through. Leave to infuse for 1 hour. Sprinkle with the toasted sesame seeds and serve.

## POMMES DE TERRE AUX HERBES

*Freshly picked herbs make all the difference to this dish. I grow my own (and anyone with a window-ledge can do the same), but I find that in the warmer regions of France, most herbs are generally far more strongly flavoured than they are at home. Be generous with them – this dish should be almost like a salad that can be enjoyed hot or cold.*

Preparation: 20 minutes
Cooking: 35 minutes

Serves 6

800g waxy potatoes
4 tbsp olive oil
3 cloves of garlic, crushed, peeled and
    chopped
1 shallot, finely diced
3 sprigs chervil, chopped
3 sprigs flat-leaf parsley, chopped
3 sprigs tarragon, chopped
slim bunch of chives, chopped
sea salt
freshly ground black pepper

Steam the potatoes for 20 minutes, and when just cool enough to handle, cut into quarters. Heat the olive oil in a large frying pan over a medium heat, add the potatoes and sauté on each side until golden, about 10–12 minutes. Remove and drain on kitchen paper. Pour away any excess oil. Add the garlic and shallot and sauté for 2 minutes over a low heat, then add the herbs and return the potatoes. Season, mix and serve.

## POMMES À L'AUVERGNATE

*This is a traditional method of preparing potatoes from the central Auvergne region, and should be made with very young Cantal cheese (although at a pinch you can use Tomme cheeses, or any other semi-hard variety). The result is a rich and succulent dish with a glossy, firm texture.*

Preparation: 15 minutes
Cooking: 20 minutes

Serves 6

1kg floury potatoes, such as Desirée or
    King Edward's
2 cloves of garlic, crushed and peeled
50g butter
4 tbsp milk
sea salt
freshly ground black pepper
400g Cantal cheese, grated or thinly
    sliced

Boil the potatoes and garlic for 20 minutes, drain well, then return to the pan and place on a low heat. Shake the pan to steam off the excess moisture for a few minutes. Remove from the heat and mash the potatoes and garlic until very smooth (a potato ricer produces the best results), then add the butter, milk and seasoning. Beat well. Add the cheese and beat vigorously for 5 minutes until all the cheese has melted to form a rich, elastic mixture. Serve at once.

## POMMES DE TERRE AUX TRUFFES

*This ultra-luxurious way of dressing up the humble potato relies on the earthy flavours of goose fat and truffle for best effect. In the south-west, where factory farming has never really managed to gain a stranglehold over the region, many farmers are now replanting truffle oaks in the place of maize and oilseed rape, with the result that, in season, fresh truffles are now increasingly affordable. If you can't get them, try a few wild mushrooms and a drizzle of truffle oil.*

Preparation: 15 minutes
Cooking: 25 minutes

Serves 6

800g waxy potatoes
20g truffle, whole or shavings
4 tbsp goose fat or olive oil
bunch of flat-leaf parsley, chopped
sea salt
freshly ground black pepper
1 tbsp truffle oil, optional

Steam the potatoes for 20 minutes, and when just cool enough to handle, cut into 4cm slices. If using a whole truffle, slice as finely as possible, and if using shavings, dice finely. Heat the goose fat (if you're a vegetarian, use a rich, fruity olive oil instead) in a large frying pan and, when hot, add the potatoes, truffle, parsley and seasoning, and fry over a medium heat for 5 minutes. Serve – making sure that you gather all the truffle pieces and parsley from the bottom of the pan. Drizzle with the truffle oil, if using.

## POMMES DE TERRE AUX CÈPES

*Once more, goose fat is a key ingredient in this dish, giving a wonderful richness to the crispy fried potatoes and complementing the fruity flavour of the cèpes. Vegetarians might try walnut oil or one of the richer varieties of olive oil instead of the goose fat – they work just as well.*

Preparation: 15 minutes
Cooking: 40 minutes

Serves 6

800g waxy potatoes
4 large cèpes, cleaned
2 tbsp goose fat, walnut oil or olive oil
2 cloves of garlic, crushed, peeled and
   chopped
sea salt
freshly ground black pepper
bunch of flat-leaf parsley, chopped

Steam the potatoes for 20 minutes, and when just cool enough to handle, cut into 4cm slices. Slice the cèpes, both cap and stalk. Heat the goose fat in a large frying pan and, when hot, add the potatoes and cèpes and cook until golden. Reduce the heat, add the garlic and cook for a further minute. Season, stir in the parsley and serve.

## HARICOTS VARIÉS À LA CIBOULETTE

*The simple spring vegetables in this dish make a terrific accompaniment to roast lamb, steamed fish or creamy gratin dauphinois.*

Preparation: 30 minutes
Cooking: 5 minutes

Serves 6

**Choose 700g in total from a selection of
the following vegetables: broad beans,
peas, French beans, runner beans,
mangetout, sugar snap
large bunch of mint
large bunch of chives
100g butter
sea salt
freshly ground black pepper**

Heat a large pan of water to boiling, then cook the prepared vegetables for 3 minutes. Drain well. Strip the mint leaves from the stems and chop finely, along with the chives. Melt the butter in a large pan. Add the drained vegetables to the pan with the mint, chives and seasoning. Stir well and serve.

# ARTICHAUTS AU VIN BLANC

*Young, sweet artichokes are one of the delights of early summer. This recipe keeps their shapes more or less intact, but adds white wine, herbs and butter for a luxurious, special treatment. Small, new season artichokes are best. If using larger ones, increase the cooking time and test by inserting a knife into the middle (they should be soft when cooked).*

Preparation: 30 minutes
Cooking: 40 minutes

Serves 6

12 small artichokes
3 cloves of garlic, crushed, peeled and
    chopped
bunch of flat-leaf parsley, chopped
12 sprigs of thyme
6 tbsp olive oil
sea salt
freshly ground black pepper
200ml white wine
100g butter

Heat the oven to 160°C/gas 3. Remove the stalk from the base of each artichoke and remove the outer leaves. Cut the tops off about halfway down and remove the inner choke with a teaspoon (if the artichokes are really small and tender this will not be necessary). Place in a baking dish, then add the garlic, herbs, olive oil and seasoning to the centre of each artichoke, pour in the white wine and cover with tin foil, twisting it around the edge of the baking dish to seal tightly. Place in the oven and cook for 35 minutes, until tender.

Remove the artichokes and heat the cooking juices. When boiling, add the butter and simmer rapidly until reduced by half. Spoon into the centre of each artichoke and serve with crusty bread.

## PETITES COURGETTES FARCIES

*Fran and I loved the shapes and colours of these beautiful little tubby courgettes. When young they have a dense texture, which holds its shape well when cooked, and a sweet, delicate flavour that contrasts nicely with the smoked lardons. If you're a vegetarian and not using lardons, make sure you compensate accordingly with a generous scatter of sea salt, which will enhance the subtle taste.*

Preparation: 20 minutes
Cooking: 50 minutes

Serves 6

6 round courgettes
2 tbsp olive oil
4 shallots, finely diced
3 cloves of garlic, crushed, peeled and
    diced
200g lardons, diced
bunch of marjoram, leaves chopped
zest and juice of 1 unwaxed lemon
freshly ground black pepper

Heat the oven to 180°C/gas 4.

Cut a lid from the stem end of each of the courgettes and scoop out the flesh to about ³/₄cm thick. Dice the flesh of the courgettes and place in a bowl. Heat a little oil in a pan, add the shallots, garlic and lardons and cook for 5 minutes over a medium heat. Stir into the courgette flesh and add the marjoram, lemon zest, pepper and lemon juice. Divide the mixture between the courgettes, then place on a lightly oiled baking sheet and top with their lids. Place in the oven and cook for 45 minutes.

## POIVRONS FARCIS

*This dish is a fine excuse to wander a summer market in search of the plumpest, the ripest, the most colourful selection of vegetables. Fat peppers, gleaming aubergines, exotically patterned courgettes and tomatoes – these ingredients are a joy to handle and to look at as well as to eat, so you can afford to be as lavish and creative as you like.*

Preparation: 30 minutes
Cooking: 1 hour 30 minutes

Serves 6

2 red onions
2 medium aubergines
2 courgettes
6 tbsp olive oil, plus extra for drizzling
6 red peppers
4 large tomatoes
3 cloves of garlic, crushed and peeled
1 red chilli
sea salt
freshly ground black pepper
3 sprigs of thyme

Heat the oven to 180°C/gas 4. Chop the onions, aubergines and courgettes into 2–3cm dice. Place in a large baking dish, pour over the olive oil, making sure all the vegetables are coated, then transfer to the oven. Roast for 30 minutes, stirring the vegetables halfway through to ensure even cooking.

Meanwhile, cut the red peppers in half lengthways and remove the seeds. Chop the tomatoes and dice the garlic and chilli. Place the tomatoes, garlic and chilli in a large bowl, season and add the thyme leaves, then mix well. When the vegetables are roasted, remove them and add them to the tomatoes. Reduce the oven temperature to 160°C/gas 3. Place the peppers cut-side up on a roasting tray and generously spoon the vegetable mix into the cavities. Drizzle with a little olive oil, place in the oven and cook for a further hour until they have reached a soft and melting consistency.

# NAVETS AU VIN BLANC

*This recipe calls for small, tender young turnips that can be cooked whole to preserve their natural sweetness.*

Preparation: 10 minutes
Cooking: 20 minutes

Serves 6

600g small turnips
30g butter
20g sugar
bunch of flat-leaf parsley, chopped
sea salt
freshly ground black pepper
50ml white wine

Wash the turnips and place in a pan with the butter and sugar, plus just enough water to cover. (If you are using larger turnips, peel and cut the turnips into wedges first.) Bring to the boil and simmer for 20 minutes, stirring from time to time. Add a little more water if necessary. Add the parsley, seasoning and wine. Simmer until almost all the liquid has evaporated, then serve.

## AUBERGINE AU GRATIN

*The irresistible texture and glossy sheen of fresh, plump aubergines is always enough to tempt me into buying. Fran suggests this as an accompaniment to roast lamb, and it's also substantial enough to eat on its own.*

Preparation: 30 minutes
Cooking: 1½ hours

Serves 6

2 cloves of garlic
6 tbsp olive oil
600g aubergines
700g tomatoes
sea salt
freshly ground black pepper
4 sprigs of thyme
100ml vegetable stock

Heat the oven to 180°C/gas 4. Rub an earthenware baking dish (about 25cm by 25cm) with one of the cloves of garlic and 1 tablespoon of the olive oil. Chop the remaining clove of garlic. Slice the aubergines and tomatoes. Put all the ends in the bottom of the dish and arrange the remaining slices on top in alternate layers, seasoning and sprinkling with garlic and thyme leaves as you go. When all the vegetables have been used up, pour over the stock, drizzle with the remaining olive oil and place in the oven to bake for 45 minutes. Reduce the heat to 160°C/gas 3 and cook for a further 45 minutes.

## CAROTTES AUX POIREAUX

*The braising method used for this dish of carrots and leeks gives them a very tender, silky consistency, and the white wine infuses the carrots with a flavour that will increase as the dish is reheated.*

Preparation: 20 minutes
Cooking: 40 minutes

Serves 6

6 carrots
5 leeks
75g butter
2 cloves of garlic, crushed, peeled and
    chopped
1 shallot, chopped
2 sprigs of thyme
2 bay leaves
sea salt
freshly ground black pepper
300ml white wine

Heat the oven to 200°C/gas 6. Clean and trim the carrots and leeks. Cut the carrots in half lengthways and cut the leeks into 5cm lengths. Melt the butter in a roasting pan; add the garlic and shallot and sauté for 1 minute. Add the prepared carrots and leeks along with the herbs, and stir well to coat with butter. Sauté for 2 minutes. Add the seasoning and wine, cover and cook in the oven for 30 minutes. Serve at once, or reheat to serve later.

93

# BETTES DU VIGNERON

*It's difficult to resist huge colourful bunches of chard with their white or red stems and big, dark-green leaves. This vegetable is more commonly cooked in water, but I find this dilutes its flavour. In this dish, the method of quick preparation keeps the flavour and colour intact and gives the chard a firm, meaty texture.*

Preparation: 20 minutes
Cooking: 10 minutes

Serves 6

1.5kg chard
2 tbsp olive oil
1 onion, chopped
1 clove of garlic, crushed, peeled and
   chopped
sea salt
freshly ground black pepper
70g pine nuts, toasted
100g raisins
½ lemon

Trim the green leaves from the chard stems, chop the leaves roughly and place to one side. Peel the strings away from the lengths of the stems (as with celery) and chop the stems into 5cm lengths. Heat the olive oil, add the onion and prepared stems, then sauté for 5 minutes and add the garlic, green leaves and seasoning. Cook on a high heat for 2 minutes, stirring constantly. Add the pine nuts and raisins, mix and serve with a squeeze of lemon juice.

## BROCCOLI AUX ANCHOIS

*Purple sprouting broccoli only ever seems to be with us for about two weeks a year, so it's essential to make the most of this wonderful vegetable while it's in season. This recipe relies on quick steaming to ensure that none of the bright colour and firm texture of the broccoli is lost; and the anchovies and lemon add just enough of a contrast to enhance, rather than overwhelm, the delicate flavour.*

Preparation: 15 minutes
Cooking: 5 minutes

Serves 6

400g purple sprouting broccoli, trimmed
100g anchovy fillets
1 red chilli
zest and juice of 1 unwaxed lemon
sea salt
freshly ground black pepper
olive oil

Steam the broccoli for 4 minutes. Cut the anchovy fillets into thin lengths, slice the chilli very finely and place in a bowl with the lemon zest and juice, seasoning and olive oil. Add the broccoli, mix well and serve.

## LÉGUMES RÔTIS SUR PETITS TOASTS

*This colourful and adaptable vegetarian dish works equally well hot or cold, as a snack, a starter or a main course with salad. The trick is in the efficient cooking of all the vegetables. The oven must be hot so that they roast quickly and retain their individual textures and colours.*

Preparation: 15 minutes
Cooking: 35 minutes

Serves 6

2 onions
3 courgettes
2 red peppers, cored
2 aubergines
4 tbsp olive oil
6 slices sourdough bread
2 cloves of garlic, peeled
sea salt
**freshly ground black pepper**

Heat the oven to 190°C/gas 5. Cut the onions into wedges and the remaining vegetables into roughly 4cm chunks. Put in a large roasting tin, coat with the olive oil and place in the hot oven. Roast for 25 minutes, then take them out, mix them up (to ensure even cooking) and return to the oven for a further 10 minutes. Meanwhile, toast the sourdough and rub with the garlic. Take the vegetables out of the oven, season and serve with the warm garlic toasts.

## POIREAUX AU POIVRON ROUGE

*The balsamic vinegar in this dish adds just a touch of spicy sweetness to the subtly flavoured colourful vegetables. Great with steamed or baked fish, chicken or with a main course potato bake.*

Preparation: 20 minutes
Cooking: 20 minutes

Serves 6

3 red peppers
4 leeks
1 tbsp olive oil
sprig of rosemary
1–2 cloves of garlic, crushed, peeled and chopped
200ml vegetable stock
2 tbsp balsamic vinegar
1 tsp sugar

Cut the peppers in half, remove the stem and seeds and chop roughly. Cut the leeks into 5cm pieces. Heat the olive oil in a large saucepan, add the vegetables and sauté for 5 minutes on a high heat, then reduce the heat, add the rosemary, garlic and stock, cover and simmer for 10 minutes. Remove the lid and increase the heat until the liquid has evaporated. Stir in the balsamic vinegar and sugar, and serve.

## CITROUILLE AU ROMARIN

*It's great to have some other excuse to buy a pumpkin than to make Hallowe'en lanterns. I grow them – they look great in the vegetable patch – but markets sell excellent ones in season. Smaller pumpkins taste sweeter and have firm, luminous orange flesh, but I avoid the very large ones that tend towards stringiness. Vegetarians can omit the lardons – just add a little extra seasoning to compensate, or a dash of chilli oil at the end.*

Preparation: 20 minutes
Cooking: 30 minutes

Serves 6

1kg pumpkin
4 tbsp olive oil, plus a little extra
4 sprigs of rosemary
sea salt
freshly ground black pepper
200g lardons

Heat the oven to 200°C/gas 6.
   Wash the pumpkin then cut it up into pieces approximately 5cm by 5cm. (Do not discard the seeds – they are delicious roasted.) Place the chopped pumpkin in a large bowl and add the olive oil. Strip the rosemary leaves from the stalks, chop finely and add to the pumpkin, along with seasoning and the lardons. Mix well. Oil a large roasting tray and place in the oven to heat for 5 minutes. Add the pumpkin and roast for 30 minutes.

## FENOUIL RÔTI

*Roasting the fennel in this way gives it an irresistible sweetness without destroying its fresh and subtle aniseed taste. For best results, and to ensure the fennel cooks evenly, use a large ovenproof dish and arrange the fennel pieces in a single layer.*

Preparation: 10 minutes
Cooking: 30 minutes

Serves 6

100g butter
2 or 3 fennel bulbs, trimmed
200ml vegetable stock
100g unrefined brown sugar
2 tbsp white wine vinegar
5 sprigs of thyme

Heat the oven to 180°C/gas 5. Melt the butter in a large ovenproof pan on the hob. Cut the fennel into quarters or halves depending on size, and cook on each side until golden. Add the stock, sugar, vinegar and thyme, bring to the boil, then bake in the oven for 25 minutes.

# LENTILLES DU PUY

*These are by far the best kind of lentils for this slow-cooking dish. Dark in colour and plump in consistency, they retain and intensify the rich flavours of the wine and herbs, with a result that can be enjoyed on its own or as a perfect accompaniment to a piece of spiced roast pork or a roast chicken.*

Preparation: 15 minutes
Cooking: 1 hour and 10 minutes

Serves 6

4 tbsp olive oil
2 red onions, sliced
2 cloves of garlic, crushed, peeled and
    chopped
400g can chopped tomatoes
1 bay leaf
4 sprigs of oregano
2 sprigs of rosemary
sea salt
freshly ground black pepper
400g Puy lentils
500ml red wine
200ml water

Heat the oven to 180°C/gas 4. Heat the oil in a large ovenproof pan on the hob. Add the onions and garlic and sauté for 5 minutes. Add the tomatoes, bay leaf, oregano, rosemary, seasoning, lentils, red wine and water. Mix well, bring to the boil, then place in the oven to bake for 30 minutes. Check and stir, then return to the oven for a further 30 minutes. By now the wine should have evaporated, allowing the Puy lentils to absorb the rich flavours.

## TOURTE AU CAMEMBERT

*This lovely combination of fresh seasonal vegetables, floury potato and golden, creamy Camembert topping makes an excellent vegetarian main course for a miserable winter's day.*

Preparation: 25 minutes
Cooking: 1 hour

Serves 6

700g potatoes
200g savoy cabbage, diced
1 clove of garlic, crushed, peeled and
    chopped
1–2 green chillies, diced
sea salt
freshly ground black pepper
1 egg, beaten
5 tbsp olive oil
200g cherry tomatoes
150g Camembert, finely sliced

Heat the oven to 180°C/gas 4. Cook the potatoes for 15 minutes, then drain and, when cool enough, cut into 3cm cubes and place in a bowl. Add the diced cabbage, garlic, chilli, seasoning and egg, and mix well. Oil a metal baking dish with some of the olive oil and place in the oven to heat. Add the remaining oil to the potato mixture. Remove the baking dish from the oven, spoon in the potato mixture, add the tomatoes and top with the finely sliced Camembert. Bake for 45 minutes until golden.

# Fish

We had to move slightly further afield for these fish recipes, to Aveyron and the Atlantic coast, which, though only a couple of hours' drive away from the Baïse, already demonstrates a completely different set of culinary traditions. This intense gastronomic regionalization is one of the joys of rural France, and to truly appreciate its diversity you need to embrace wholeheartedly the various specialities of each region. To choose to eat steak in Aveyron would be as perverse as to try to buy fish in Nérac. The markets reflect this: all Fran and I had to do to collect our fish recipes was to visit them, talk to the locals, and allow temptation to have its way.

Freshly caught fish is essential for these recipes, so make sure you choose fish with bright eyes, shiny, colourful scales and no strong odour. Good, fresh fish should always feel firm and have bright red, healthy gills. Your fishmonger should be able to gut and fillet any fish for you, but if you prefer to do the job yourself, ensure your filleting knife is as sharp as possible. Keep your fish in the coolest part of the fridge under damp paper, and always cook it on the day of purchase.

## FRUITS DE MER À L'AÏOLI

*The only skill involved in creating this spectacular and sociable dish is that of choosing the freshest and most delicious local ingredients. We've used razor clams here, which are abundant on the Atlantic coast, and palourdes, a generous-sized shellfish with a characteristic hazelnut flavour. You can afford to be flexible, however – and remember that if you choose what's in season and what has been caught locally, you can't go far wrong. Serve with a green salad.*

Preparation: 20 minutes
Cooking: 15 minutes

Serves 6

1 recipe quantity aïoli (see page 52)
1kg palourdes
6 razor clams
6 crab claws
6 scallops
400g large uncooked tiger prawns
3 cloves of garlic, crushed, peeled and
    chopped
4 tbsp olive oil
2 chillies, chopped
3 sprigs of rosemary
large bunch of parsley
large bunch of basil
sea salt
freshly ground black pepper

Make the aïoli as on page 52. If you want to make this in advance, cover it with cling film, making sure the film touches the aïoli and excludes any air. This will stop a skin forming.

Place the palourdes and razor clams in a large bowl of cold water and soak for 10 minutes. Rinse and repeat. This removes any sand from the shells.

Heat the oven to 200°C/gas 6. Place the palourdes, razor clams, crab claws, scallops and tiger prawns in a large bowl. Add the garlic, olive oil and chillies. Strip the rosemary leaves from the twigs, chop them and add to the seafood. Mix well, then pour onto a large roasting pan and place in the oven to roast for 15 minutes, checking halfway through that everything is cooking evenly.

Strip the leaves from the parsley and basil and chop or tear. When the shellfish are cooked, sprinkle with the herbs and seasoning and serve with the aïoli.

# BOUQUET AU CITRON

*This is really such a simple dish that it hardly counts as a recipe at all – although it's still my all-time favourite seaside picnic dish. In France, cooked prawns are available at roadside stalls all down the coast, of course, but nothing beats the freshest, sweetest Atlantic prawns, served with lemon, lime and a glass of chilled Muscadet …*

Preparation: 5 minutes
Cooking: 5 minutes

Serves 6

2kg large prawns, raw
3 lemons, cut into wedges
3 limes, cut into wedges

Heat a large pan of water and, when boiling rapidly, add all the prawns. Bring back to the boil, cover and simmer for 2 minutes. Drain and refresh under cold water and chill in a colander in the fridge. Serve with the lemons and limes.

# HUÎTRES AUX LARDONS

*Having been brought up on raw oysters (where my family comes from it's considered sacrilege to eat oysters any other way), I was at first rather suspicious of this dish. Having tried it, however, I have to say it's pretty good. Just don't tell my mother …*

Preparation: 30 minutes
Cooking: 4 minutes

Serves 6

36 oysters
12 slices bacon, finely chopped
3 cloves of garlic, crushed, peeled and chopped
bunch of parsley, finely chopped
freshly ground black pepper

Open the oysters with a small, sharp knife. Place them in their shells on a grill pan. Do not overcrowd the grill pan – it is best to cook the oysters in batches. Mix together the bacon, garlic and parsley and season with pepper. Divide between the oysters, sprinkling over the top, then place under the grill and cook for 3–4 minutes until the oysters are bubbling and the bacon is sizzling.

# SEICHE FARCIE

*This recipe is a speciality of Sète, a beautiful village
on the Mediterranean with canals running through
the streets. Use medium or large squid (seiche) for
this unusual combination of sea and land
ingredients.*

Preparation: 30 minutes
Cooking: 20 minutes

Serves 6

12 medium-sized squid without tentacles,
 about 450g total weight
2 tbsp olive oil
2 cloves of garlic, crushed, peeled and
 chopped
200g minced pork
bunch of parsley, finely chopped
bunch of oregano, finely chopped
50g pistachios, chopped
sea salt
freshly ground black pepper
40g breadcrumbs
1 egg
4 tbsp olive oil
200ml white wine

Check that the squid have been properly
cleaned and have no thin transparent film on
them. Heat the oil in a pan and add the garlic
and pork. Cook over a medium heat for 5
minutes, using a wooden spoon to break up
the meat. Remove from the heat and add the
parsley, oregano, pistachios, seasoning and
breadcrumbs. Mix well. Beat the egg and add
to the mixture, stirring through until the
mixture combines.

Using a small spoon, stuff each squid with
this mixture (taking care not to overfill). Leave
about 3cm empty at the open end of each
squid to allow the stuffing to expand. Heat
some olive oil in a large frying pan and fry the
squid on all sides until golden brown (about
8 minutes). Remove from the pan and keep
warm. Add the white wine to the pan, bring
to a rapid boil and cook until reduced by half.
Pour over the squid and serve at once.

VILLE DE LÈGE - CAP FERRET

*La Pointe est fragile.*

## SALADE DE CALAMARS

*This warm squid salad is so quick and easy to make that it seems almost criminal to opt for the rubbery ready-cooked stuff you can buy in jars. Prepared fresh, the squid is creamy and tender on the inside, golden on the outside, and is irresistible served hot over the zesty salad dressing.*

Preparation: 20 minutes
Cooking: 2 minutes

Serves 6

1 seasonal lettuce, washed
150g rocket
4 tbsp olive oil
zest and juice of 1 unwaxed lemon
sea salt
freshly ground black pepper
2 cloves of garlic, crushed, peeled and
    finely chopped
bunch of flat-leaf parsley, finely chopped
bunch of lemon thyme, finely chopped
600g small squid, cleaned
2 tbsp olive oil

Break the lettuce into pieces in a large salad bowl, and add the rocket leaves. Mix together the olive oil, lemon juice and seasoning in a small bowl and place to one side.

Combine the finely chopped garlic, parsley, thyme and lemon zest. Check that the squid have been properly cleaned and have no thin transparent film on them. Separate the tentacles and cut the body into rings. Heat the oil until very hot, then add the squid (along with its tentacles) and cook for 1 minute on a high heat, tossing constantly. Add the garlic mixture and cook for a further minute.

Pour the dressing over the salad and mix well. Add the hot squid and serve at once.

## SALADE DE CRABE À L'AVOCAT

*This delicious combination of sweet crab and creamy avocado is perfect for a summer picnic or light lunch. Purists may prefer to cook their own crab, but most fishmongers should have ready-cooked fresh crabs and freshly prepared crab meat, which, as long as it has not been frozen, should serve just as well.*

Preparation: 20 minutes

Serves 6

700g white crabmeat
200g brown crabmeat
3 spring onions
1 red chilli
juice of 2 limes
sea salt
freshly ground black pepper
300g small new-season tomatoes
50g toasted sesame seeds
3 tbsp olive oil
1 small lettuce, washed
3 avocados

Mix the crabmeat, spring onions, chilli, lime juice and seasoning in a bowl. Cut the tomatoes in half and place in a bowl with the toasted sesame seeds, seasoning and olive oil. Lay a bed of lettuce leaves on each of the serving plates, cut the avocados in half and remove the stones, peel and place on top of the lettuce. Divide the crabmeat between the avocados, filling the hollows generously, then add the sesame tomatoes to the plates and serve at once.

## SOLE VAPEUR

*The chervil in the lemon-and-oil dressing gives the steamed sole a distinctive, unusual, aromatic freshness.*

Preparation: 20 minutes
Cooking: 5 minutes

Serves 6

bunch of chives
bunch of chervil
6 tbsp olive oil
zest and juice of 2 unwaxed lemons
sea salt
freshly ground black pepper
6 x 150g skinned sole fillets
6 baby leeks
100g asparagus
100g sugar snap peas
100g broad beans

Chop the chives and chervil, then mix with the olive oil, lemon zest and juice and seasoning. Set aside. Prepare a steamer, brush with oil and place on the heat to boil the water. Roll the sole fillets up into neat little logs and place in the steamer (when the water is simmering), making sure that the final fold is underneath to keep them rolled while cooking. Add the leeks and steam for 3 minutes. Add the asparagus, sugar snaps and broad beans and cook for a further 2 minutes. Carefully remove the fish and vegetables and serve with the herb and lemon oil spooned over the fish.

## BARBUE AU THYM

*With really good ingredients, a recipe can be as simple as you like. This recipe makes the most of a delicious sea fish whilst not overpowering its flavour. Enjoy with a salad or a few steamed vegetables for the authentic taste of the Atlantic.*

Preparation: 15 minutes, plus an hour's
    marinating
Cooking: 8 minutes

Serves 6

6 x 160g brill fillets
large bunch of thyme
1 clove of garlic, crushed, peeled and
    chopped
zest of 1 lemon
4 tbsp olive oil
sea salt
freshly ground black pepper

Dry the brill with kitchen paper. Chop the thyme leaves finely, discarding the stems. Combine the thyme with the garlic, lemon zest, olive oil and seasoning in a dish big enough to take the brill. Add the brill to the marinade and with your hands coat it all over. Cover and leave to marinate for at least an hour in the fridge. When ready to cook, heat the grill to high. Place the fish on a grill rack and cook for 4 minutes on each side.

## MAQUEREAU À LA DIJONNAISE

*Gleaming, fresh blue mackerel are one of the
Atlantic's greatest treasures, prepared here with
young leeks and Dijon mustard for a subtle
combination of flavours and textures.*

Preparation: 15 minutes
Cooking: 12 minutes

Serves 6

6 mackerel, filleted
2 tbsp Dijon mustard
bunch of oregano, chopped
sea salt
freshly ground black pepper
olive oil for drizzling
2 young leeks
1 tsp coriander seeds, crushed

Heat the oven to 200°C/gas 6. Score the skin
side of the mackerel fillets with a sharp knife.
Turn the fillets over and spread the flesh with
the Dijon mustard, then sprinkle with the
oregano and season to taste.

Oil a roasting tray and arrange six of the
fillets on it, skin-side down. Trim and slice the
leeks very finely and place on the six fillets.
Sprinkle with the coriander seeds, season
again, then place a fillet on top of each one,
making a sandwich. Drizzle with a little
olive oil and roast in the top of the oven for
12 minutes.

## MULLET AU POIVRON ROUGE

*There are few fish on the French market as beautiful and enticing as the red mullet. This recipe spices it up with chillies and sweet red peppers for a simple but elegant light meal.*

Preparation: 10 minutes
Cooking: 25 minutes

Serves 6

4 tbsp olive oil
2 red onions, sliced
2 red peppers, cut into strips
3 cloves of garlic, crushed, peeled and
   chopped
1 chilli, finely chopped
1 tbsp white wine vinegar
50ml fish stock
sea salt
freshly ground black pepper
100g flour
6 x 160g red mullet fillets

Heat 2 tablespoons of the oil in a pan. Add the onion and pepper and sauté for 5 minutes, then add the garlic and chilli and cook for a further 2 minutes without burning. Reduce the heat, pour in the vinegar and stock and cook gently for 10 minutes.

Season the flour on a plate. Dip the fillets in and dust all over. Heat the remaining olive oil in a large pan and cook the fillets for 3 minutes on each side. Serve at once with the spicy sauce.

## SAUMON AU CHAMPAGNE

*This is a spectacular celebratory dish, perfect for using up that last glass of flat champagne (or a perfect excuse for opening another bottle). It's easy to make, too, which means you can dazzle your guests with your conversation as well as with your cooking …*

Preparation: 10 minutes
Cooking: 20 minutes

Serves 6

50g butter
3 banana shallots, finely chopped
6 x 160g salmon steaks
400ml champagne or sparkling white wine
100ml double cream
sea salt
freshly ground black pepper
bunch of dill, chopped

Melt the butter in a broad, low-sided pan, then add the shallots and sauté for 3 minutes. Arrange the salmon steaks over the shallots in a single layer, then add the champagne and simmer, covered, for 8 minutes. Remove the salmon and keep warm. Boil the sauce rapidly until it has reduced by half. Add the cream and simmer for 5 minutes until it has reached a coating consistency, then season, add the dill and serve the salmon steaks with the sauce spooned over them.

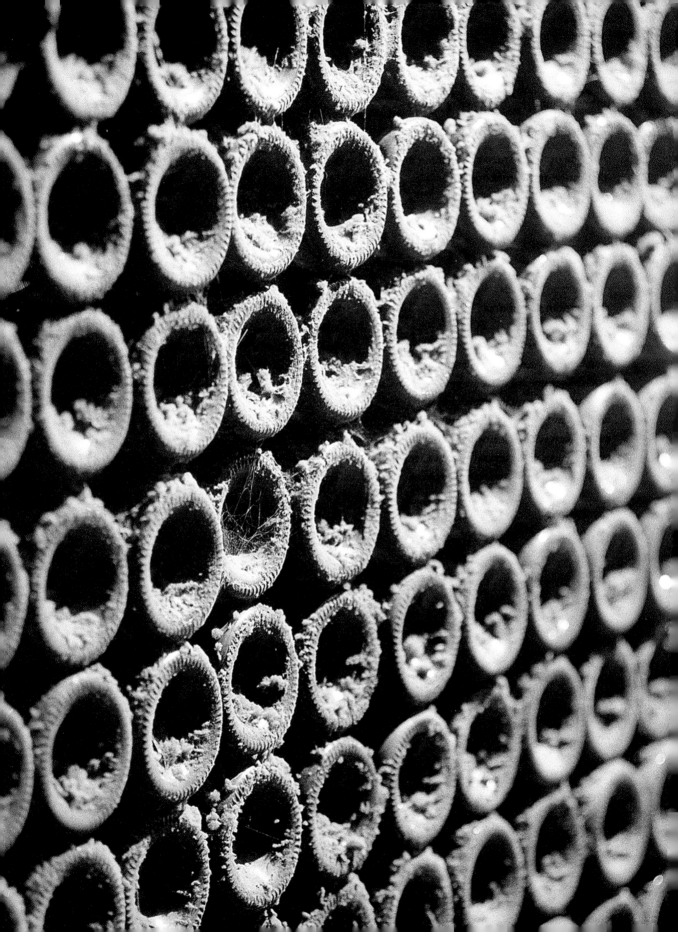

# DAURADE AU VIN BLANC

*This dish relies principally on the freshness of its ingredients, and the white wine infuses the young vegetables with a heady yet delicate flavour.*

Preparation: 15 minutes
Cooking: 25 minutes

Serves 6

6 x 160g John Dory or sea bass fillets
450g baby new-season carrots, peeled
300ml white wine, plus a little extra if
   needed
6 sprigs of thyme
2 bay leaves
4 tbsp olive oil
300g new-season green peas, shelled
600g asparagus, trimmed
4 tbsp olive oil
sea salt
freshly ground black pepper

Heat the oven to 220°C/gas 7. Remove excess bones from the fish, then dry the fish with kitchen paper. Score the skin with a sharp knife to stop the fillets curling while cooking.

Place the carrots, wine and herbs in a large baking dish, cover with a lid or sheet of baking paper or foil folded into place, and place in the oven to cook for 15 minutes.

Heat the olive oil in a large frying pan, then cook the fillets skin-side down for 1 minute. Turn and cook for another minute. Cook the fish in batches, keeping the pan really hot to seal in the juices. As soon as all the fish is seared, take the carrots out of the oven and add the fish, skin-side up. Add more wine if necessary. Add the peas and asparagus to the dish, drizzle with olive oil and baste the vegetables and fish with the wine and oil. Return to the oven without any cover and roast for 7 minutes. Season, and serve the fish with the vegetables and any remaining juices.

## TRUITE DE MER SAUCE VERTE

*The fresh green sauce complements the grilled sea bream perfectly in this tangy, summer dish. Serve the fish, if you like, on a bed of ribbon pasta with grilled tomato halves.*

Preparation: 20 minutes
Cooking: 10 minutes

Serves 6

6 x filleted sea bream (500g each before
    filleting)
1 clove of garlic, crushed, peeled and
    chopped
100g pitted green olives
bunch of parsley
bunch of tarragon
40g capers, chopped
juice of 1 lemon
100ml olive oil
2 tbsp white wine vinegar
freshly ground black pepper

Dry the fish with kitchen paper, and score the skin to stop the fillets curling up. Heat the grill to high, oil a baking tray and arrange the fillets skin-side up. Cook for 5 minutes. Meanwhile, put the remaining ingredients in a blender and blitz, or chop finely and combine into a sauce. Turn the fish, cook for a further 2 minutes and serve at once with the freshly made sauce.

# TURBOT AUX CREVETTES ROSES

*In his* Grand Dictionnaire de Cuisine, *Dumas maintains that the combination of turbot and prawns is a typically English dish – all I can say is that the French must have taken it back since then without anyone noticing!*

Preparation: 20 minutes
Cooking: 15 minutes

Serves 6

6 x 180–200g turbot fillets or steaks
4 tbsp olive oil
sea salt
freshly ground black pepper
3 bay leaves
3 sprigs of thyme
100g butter
6 unpeeled raw prawns
100g peeled raw prawns
3 cloves of garlic, crushed, peeled and
    chopped
juice of 2 lemons
bunch of flat-leaf parsley, chopped

Heat the oven to 220°C/gas 7. Dry the fish with kitchen paper. Oil a large roasting pan with the olive oil and put in the turbot with the seasoning, bay leaves and thyme. Place in the oven and roast for 15 minutes. Melt the butter in a pan, then add the whole prawns and sauté for 5 minutes. Add the peeled prawns and garlic and sauté for a further 2 minutes. When the turbot is cooked, add the lemon juice and parsley to the prawns, then spoon the mixture over the turbot and serve.

# TRUITE À L'ÉTOUFFÉE

*This is the perfect way to prevent trout from losing its tenderness in the oven, and it can be adapted for almost any fish (red snapper, salmon, John Dory, sea bream, and so on). The variations are endless – try experimenting with capers, salicorne (the pickled seaweed condiment so popular all down the Atlantic coast), or adding prawns and a spoonful of crème fraîche.*

Preparation: 30 minutes
Cooking: 20 minutes

Serves 6

6 sheets baking paper or foil
12 cooked potatoes
2 shallots, finely chopped
2 cloves of garlic, crushed, peeled and
   chopped
sea salt
freshly ground black pepper
2 leeks, chopped
6 whole trout, cleaned
6 sprigs of thyme
100ml white wine
25g butter
1 lemon, cut into 6 wedges

Heat the oven to 200°C/gas 6. Lay out the large sheets of baking paper or foil. Slice the cooked potatoes and divide them between the sheets. Mix together the shallots, garlic, seasoning and leeks, then spoon the mixture onto the potatoes. Add a trout to each parcel, top with a sprig of thyme, a spoonful of wine and a knob of butter. Fold the parcels together and twist to seal securely. Lift the parcels onto baking trays and place in the oven to cook for 20 minutes. Serve in the parcels, with lemon wedges.

## THON AUX DEUX HARICOTS

*The melting consistency of the flageolet beans in this recipe makes a lovely contrast to the barely cooked, crisp green beans and just-seared tuna steaks.*

Preparation: 30 minutes
Cooking: 15 minutes

Serves 6

6 x 150g tuna steaks
200g French beans, trimmed
200g canned flageolet beans, drained
zest and juice of 1 unwaxed lemon
3 tbsp olive oil
100g pitted green olives
4 tomatoes, peeled, deseeded and chopped
1 clove of garlic, crushed, peeled and
    chopped
bunch of basil, leaves stripped from stalks
sea salt
freshly ground black pepper

Heat a griddle pan, and when it is really hot, sear the tuna in batches on each side: 2 minutes for rare, 3 for medium, 4 for well done.

Plunge the French beans into a large pan of water and cook for 2 minutes. Add the flageolets and simmer for 1 minute. Drain well and return to the pan with the lemon zest and juice, olive oil, olives, tomatoes, garlic, basil leaves and seasoning. Toss well in the warm pan, then divide between serving plates and top with the seared tuna steaks.

# SAINT-JACQUES AUX POMMES VAPEUR

*This rustic combination of fried king scallops, lardons and steamed tarragon potatoes is typical of the south-west coast, where farmers and fishermen exchange recipes as well as tall tales …*

Preparation: 20 minutes
Cooking: 25 minutes

Serves 6

600g waxy potatoes
3 tbsp olive oil
200g lardons
18 king scallops
bunch of tarragon, leaves chopped
sea salt
freshly ground black pepper
1 tbsp white wine vinegar
50g butter

Steam the potatoes for 20 minutes. Heat 1 tablespoon of the olive oil in a pan and fry the lardons for 5 minutes until crispy. If the scallops are still in their shells, open them and cut away from the shell, removing the dark thread that runs along the side of the scallop. Rinse and dry with kitchen paper.

When the potatoes are cooked and cool enough to handle, cut into thick slices, place in a bowl and add the lardons, tarragon (reserving a little for garnish), seasoning, the remaining 2 tablespoons of olive oil and the vinegar. Mix well.

In another pan, heat the butter and cook the scallops on each side for 1 minute until golden. Place on top of the potatoes and garnish with a little tarragon. Serve at once.

Serves 6

1kg monkfish tail
sea salt
freshly ground black pepper
75g plain flour
2 tbsp olive oil
50g butter
2 shallots, chopped
2 cloves of garlic, crushed, peeled and
   chopped
300g girolles, cleaned
200ml white wine
100ml cream
bunch of flat-leaf parsley, chopped

Remove all the membrane from the monkfish
(this is important, otherwise cooking will turn
it an unpleasant grey). Cut the two fillets away
from the central bone and then divide the
fillets into 6 equal pieces. Season the monkfish
and coat it evenly with the flour. In a large
shallow pan heat the olive oil and butter, then
add the fish and cook for 2 minutes on each
side. Remove the fish; add the shallots, garlic
and girolles, and cook on a low heat for 5
minutes, stirring frequently. Increase the heat,
return the monkfish to the pan, add the wine
and simmer, covered, for 5 minutes. Remove
the lid from the pan and allow the liquid to
evaporate by half. Add the cream and simmer
for 2 minutes to allow the sauce to thicken
slightly. Add the chopped parsley, and serve.

## LOTTE AUX GIROLLES

*This is a complex, luscious marriage of flavours,
rich with cream, wine and fragrant girolle
mushrooms. Serve the monkfish with something
appropriately gentle: plain rice, steamed potatoes
or simple pasta shells will complement it perfectly.*

Preparation: 20 minutes
Cooking: 25 minutes

# FLÉTAN À LA BORDELAISE

*This is an unusual way of cooking fish, full of depth and flavour. Other varieties of fish can be used, such as salmon, brill and cod, but halibut works perfectly here, gently simmered in herbs and wine.*

Preparation: 30 minutes
Cooking: 25 minutes

Serves 6

400g button onions
50g butter
300g button mushrooms
2 sprigs of thyme
2 bay leaves
1 bottle red Bordeaux wine
sea salt
freshly ground black pepper
6 x 180–200g halibut steaks
2 tsp arrowroot
bunch of flat-leaf parsley, finely chopped

Peel the onions by plunging them into boiling water for a few moments then slipping off the skins. Melt the butter in a large low-sided pan, add the mushrooms and onions and cook for 5 minutes. Add the thyme sprigs, bay leaves, wine and seasoning, and simmer gently for 5 minutes. Carefully place the halibut steaks in the pan, baste with red wine, cover and cook for about 6 minutes. When the fish is ready, the central bone will come out easily if pulled. Lift the fish out of the pan onto serving plates. With a slotted spoon, remove the onions and mushrooms and arrange on the plates with the fish. Remove the thyme and bay leaves and discard. Take the pan from the heat and add the arrowroot, mixing well, then stir in the parsley and spoon the sauce over the fish.

# Meat, Game & Poultry

For these recipes, you should consider making friends with your local organic butcher. There's really no comparison between free-range meat and the factory-produced variety, in either taste or quality. In rural French markets of the south-west, dominated as they are by speciality farmers, most meat is free-range and organic, and locals will usually point you in the direction of the best producers.

Because of the regional nature of this cookbook, you'll find that there is a greater than usual number of recipes involving game birds and poultry – pigeon, pheasant, goose and, most especially, duck. These are freely available in French markets of the south-west, and can be found at specialist butchers in Britain. Ducks and geese in France are most commonly sold as follows:

*Canard:* a duck, aged 2–4 months.
*Cane/canette:* a female duck. In his *Grand Dictionnaire de Cuisine*, Dumas makes the point that these usually have a superior taste and tenderness to the male.
*Caneton:* a duckling.
*Magret de canard:* the breast of a duck that has been traditionally fattened for foie gras. Often smoked or air-dried, when it may be carved thinly without cooking and served as part of a salad.
*Confit d'oie/de canard:* a preserve of goose or duck in its own fat.
*Gésiers confits:* duck or goose necks in *confit*, often used in salads.
*Graisse d'oie/de canard:* goose or duck fat, used for enriching soups and casseroles as well as for roasting potatoes.
*Foie gras:* liver from a traditionally fattened goose or duck.

At the market in Nérac we were lucky enough to run into Bernard Mounet, whose family have been keeping geese and ducks for generations. Foie gras is his passion, and although his farm is small, he has won many international prizes for his produce. He was pleasantly surprised at our interest in his farm. Many English, he said, are anti-foie gras; this is because they are used to factory farming, where the birds are treated badly and without respect. On his farm, as on most other small farms of the region, the birds are fed on nothing but maize and are allowed to wander freely, and the difference is not only in the taste. You have to respect the bird, says M. Mounet, to appreciate what you are eating and where it comes from.

This idea of respect and appreciation is one that lives on in farms around the region. It forms a part of the *patrimoine* – that strange French word that implies at the same time tradition, heritage, love of the land, awareness of the past. It is a love of the *patrimoine* that has kept so many of these old country recipes alive, along with the way of life that created them. All are best using organically and preferably locally farmed meat of the highest possible quality.

# AGNEAU AUX HARICOTS BLANCS

*This is a dish of strong, hearty flavours, in which the red wine, garlic, rosemary and chillies lift the mild flavour of the butter beans for a warm and delicious combination. Serve with a simple green leaf salad to follow. My great-grandmother used to make her version of this dish every year at Easter; I'm glad to see that in Gascony, too, the tradition continues…*

Preparation: 20 minutes, plus overnight
    soaking
Cooking: 2½ hours

Serves 6

250g dried butter or haricot beans, soaked
    overnight
4 tbsp olive oil
1.8kg leg of lamb (cut the shank off)
3 red onions, chopped
1 bulb of garlic, cloves crushed, peeled and
    chopped
1 bottle red wine
2 x 400g tins chopped tomatoes
300ml stock
3 sprigs of rosemary
1–2 chillies, diced
sea salt
freshly ground black pepper

Drain the butter beans and place in a pan of water. Bring to the boil, reduce the heat and simmer for 1 hour, removing any froth that comes to the surface.

Heat the oven to 180°C/gas 4.

Heat the olive oil in a large flameproof casserole. Add the lamb and cook on each side for 15 minutes until golden, then remove. Add the onions and sauté for 5 minutes, then add the garlic and cook for a further minute. Add the red wine, tomatoes, stock, rosemary, chilli, seasoning and cooked beans. Mix well and return the leg of lamb to the pot. Immerse it in the mixture, then place in the oven to cook for 1½ hours, checking occasionally.

# BOEUF BOURGUIGNON

*This is one of the best known and most typical of French dishes, and relies on a lengthy cooking time to absorb the flavour of the herbs and wine and to give the beef an irresistible tenderness. Garnish the finished dish with parsley and croûtons, if you like.*

Preparation: 30 minutes
Cooking: 2³/₄ hours

Serves 6

4 tbsp olive oil
1.4kg chuck, flank or skirt of beef, cubed
2 onions, chopped
2 cloves of garlic, crushed, peeled and
    chopped
50g plain flour
1 bottle red burgundy wine
300ml beef stock
1 tbsp tomato purée
2 sprigs of thyme
2 bay leaves
sea salt
freshly ground black pepper
200g smoked lardons
250g button onions
250g button mushrooms

Heat the oven to 180°C/gas 4.

Heat the olive oil in a large casserole. Put in just enough meat to cover the bottom of the pan and brown evenly on a high heat, then remove and repeat until all the meat is browned. Add the onions and cook for 4 minutes, then add the garlic for a further minute. Remove from the heat and sieve in the flour, mixing well to absorb all the oil. Return the pan to a low heat and slowly pour in the red wine and stock, stirring constantly. Bring to the boil. Return the meat to the casserole with the tomato purée, herbs and seasoning. Cover with a lid and cook in the oven for 2 hours.

Fry the lardons in a non-stick pan for 4 minutes, until they have released some of their fat, then add the button onions and mushrooms. Cook for about 10 minutes until golden. Add to the beef and mix in. Return to the oven to cook for a further 30 minutes.

# AGNEAU FARCI

*The roasted red peppers give a wonderful smoky sweetness to the lamb in this spectacular and colourful celebratory dish.*

Preparation: 45 minutes
Cooking: 1½–2 hours

1 x 2kg saddle of lamb, about 1.6kg when boned
2 red peppers
2 tbsp olive oil, plus extra to oil the roasting tin
2 red onions, chopped
2 cloves of garlic, crushed, peeled and chopped
1 jar artichokes, drained weight 180g, chopped
75g pitted olives, chopped
100g minced lamb
2 sprigs of rosemary, leaves chopped
sea salt
freshly ground black pepper
1 egg yolk

Heat the oven to 190°C/gas 5. Lay the lamb flat, skin-side down, and have some butcher's string ready for tying. Spear each of the peppers with a carving fork, and, over a naked flame, turn until the skin is charred and blistered. Place in a bowl and cover with cling film for 10 minutes.

Heat the oil in a frying pan and sauté the onion for 5 minutes, then add the garlic and cook for a further minute. In a bowl, combine the onion and garlic with the artichokes, olives, minced lamb, rosemary, seasoning and egg yolk. Mix well. Peel the red peppers, then cut the flesh away from the stalks, taking care to discard the seeds.

Spread the artichoke mixture evenly over the lamb, then place all the red peppers in one long strip down the middle. Roll the two sides of the saddle together and tie with string every 2.5cm to secure it. Oil a roasting tin, put in the saddle and roast for 1 hour 20 minutes for rare; add on 20 minutes for medium and another 20 minutes for well done. Remove from the oven and place in a warm place to rest for 10 minutes, then carve and serve.

# BOEUF À LA BLONDE

*The beer in this savoury recipe gives the beef
a pleasantly bittersweet edge.*

Preparation: 30 minutes
Cooking: 2 hours 20 minutes

Serves 6

4 tbsp olive oil
1.4kg topside or flank of beef, cut into
    cubes
3 onions, roughly chopped
200g bacon
2 cloves of garlic, crushed, peeled and
    chopped
20g plain flour
500ml light ale
2 sprigs of thyme
2 bay leaves
sea salt
freshly ground black pepper

Heat the oven to 180°C/gas 4.

Heat the olive oil in a large casserole pan.
Add just enough meat to cover the bottom and
brown evenly on a high heat, then remove and
repeat until all the meat is browned. Add the
onions and bacon and cook for 4 minutes.
Add the garlic and cook for a further minute.
Remove from the heat and sieve in the flour,
mixing well to absorb all the oil. Return the
pan to the heat, pour in the light ale, stirring
constantly, and bring to the boil. Return the
meat to the pan, stir and once more bring to
the boil. Add the thyme, bay leaves and
seasoning. Cover and cook in the oven for
2 hours.

## PORC AUX CHÂTAIGNES

*Traditionally made with wild boar, this is a classic winter dish: satisfyingly sweet and starchy, but full of rich flavour. It's a terrific excuse to buy the fat, glossy new chestnuts as they begin to appear on markets all over France (even better to collect them wild), although vacuum-packed or tinned chestnuts are a godsend to anyone in a hurry.*

Preparation: 15 minutes
Cooking: 2 hours

Serves 6

3 tbsp olive oil
1.4 kg skinned, boned, rolled and tied loin of pork
400g button onions or small shallots
4 cloves of garlic, crushed, peeled and chopped
400ml white wine
6 sprigs of thyme
1 bay leaf
sea salt
freshly ground black pepper
30 peeled chestnuts

Heat the oven to 180°C/gas 4. Heat the oil in an ovenproof casserole dish on the hob. Add the pork, brown evenly, then remove from the dish and put aside. Fry the whole small onions gently until brown, then add the garlic and cook for another minute. Return the pork to the dish and add the wine, herbs and seasoning. Boil rapidly for 3 minutes. Place the lid on the casserole and transfer to the oven. After 1 hour, take it out and add the chestnuts, then cook for a further 30 minutes.

To serve, carve the meat and arrange on a bed of onions and chestnuts, with the sauce.

## PORC AUX PRUNEAUX

*This is a quick and easy cold-weather dish that makes full use of the rich flavours of sizzling pork, winter apple and luscious Agen prunes.*

Preparation: 20 minutes
Cooking: 30 minutes

Serves 6

200g Agen prunes
3 cooking apples, peeled, cored and sliced
200ml white wine or chicken stock
3 red onions
olive oil for frying
sea salt
freshly ground black pepper
6 pork chops
a bunch of sage, leaves chopped
2 tbsp Armagnac

In a pan place the prunes, apples and wine or stock. Bring to the boil and simmer gently for 15 minutes so that the mixture becomes a rich apple sauce.

Cut the onions in half and cook them in oil for 8 minutes on the flat side, then turn and cook for 8 minutes on the other side, trying to keep the halves intact. Meanwhile, heat the grill. Season the chops and cook on each side for 10–12 minutes. Add the sage and Armagnac to the apple sauce. Take the chops from the grill and serve with the onions and sauce.

## FOIE GRAS AUX CHANTERELLES

*No regional French cookbook is complete without a recipe for foie gras, an ingredient that goes back to Roman times and encompasses a thousand years of French culinary history. It is an artisan product, both expensive and difficult to manufacture – so don't be tempted by the factory-farmed stuff, which has no taste and which is produced without care or respect. Specialist French markets sell the real thing, produced by hand and using traditional methods. This recipe is as simple as it gets, because when you're eating something this good, you need nothing more.*

Preparation: 15 minutes
Cooking: 15 minutes

Serves 6

75g butter
200g chanterelle mushrooms, cleaned
600g fresh foie gras, cut into six 2cm slices
6 slices brioche
sea salt
freshly ground black pepper

Heat 50g butter in a frying pan. Add the whole mushrooms and cook over a high heat for 5 minutes. Heat the remaining butter in a non-stick frying pan and, when hot, sear the foie gras on each side for 1 minute over a high heat. Toast the brioche until just golden – take care, as it browns very quickly. Top the toasted brioche with the cooked chanterelles and season to taste. Rest the cooked foie gras on top and serve at once.

## PORC AUX CÈPES

*Cèpes are one of the delights of the late-summer market. Dumas praised them in his* Grand Dictionnaire de la Cuisine *as at their best in August, carpeting the forests of Compiègne and of the Bordeaux region. This recipe is simple but effective; try it with some green beans for a quick, elegant meal on a summer evening.*

Preparation: 10 minutes
Cooking: 30 minutes

Serves 6

4 tbsp olive oil
6 pork steaks
4 large cèpes, sliced (caps and stalks)
3 cloves of garlic, crushed, peeled and chopped
6 tbsp white wine
sea salt
freshly ground black pepper
a bunch of flat-leaf parsley, chopped

Heat 2 tablespoons of the oil in a pan and fry the pork steaks for 3 minutes on each side, then reduce the heat and cook for a further 8 minutes. Meanwhile, in a second pan, heat the remaining olive oil and fry the cèpes for 4 minutes on a high heat, then reduce the heat and cook for a further 10 minutes. Add the cèpes to the pork steaks, along with the garlic and wine, and cook for 5 minutes. Season, stir in the parsley and serve.

# CASSOULET TOULOUSAIN

*This very old traditional peasant dish has a thousand variants, every one of which is considered by its followers to be the real deal. Personally, I prefer it without the breadcrumbs (although I know that in some parts of France this makes me a Philistine), and there is also some serious division of opinion regarding the tomatoes. Everyone agrees, however, that as winter comfort food goes, you can't get much better. The slow cooking time means that everything is infused with the rich flavours of the confit and the herbs, and that the beans are lusciously soft and buttery. Enjoy it with fresh country bread (pain de campagne) and a contrasting side salad, or luxuriously on its own.*

Preparation: 30 minutes, plus overnight
   soaking
Cooking: 4 hours

Serves 6 generously

400g dried haricot beans, soaked overnight
   in water, drained
200g pork rind
3 onions, 1 whole and studded with 3
   cloves
2 carrots
5 large tomatoes, peeled and quartered
1 bouquet garni
6 cloves of garlic, crushed and peeled
2 tbsp goose fat
400g boned shoulder of lamb, cut into 6
300g pork belly, cut into large cubes
several sprigs of thyme
sea salt
freshly ground black pepper
400g Toulouse sausages
400g preserved goose or duck legs (confit)
250g breadcrumbs

Place the beans in a large pot with the pork rind, whole clove-studded onion, whole carrots, quartered tomatoes, bouquet garni and 2 cloves of garlic. Cover generously with water and simmer for 1 to 2 hours until tender. Skim off any froth while cooking, and add more water if needed.

About halfway through the beans' cooking time, chop the 2 remaining onions and 3 of the remaining garlic cloves. In a large pan, heat half of the goose fat and brown the lamb, then add the onions, garlic and pork belly. Using water from the pan of beans, add just enough to cover the lamb, then add the thyme and the seasoning, cover and simmer for 1 hour.

Brown the sausages in the remaining goose fat and add to the lamb for the last 10 minutes of cooking.

Now heat the oven to 180°C/gas 4. Remove the bouquet garni, whole carrots, onion and pork rind from the bean pot and discard. Rub the inside of a large earthenware casserole dish with the last clove of garlic. Add half the beans to the pot, and on top place all the meat – including the preserved goose or duck – then cover with the remaining beans.

Bring to the boil on the stove, then lightly sprinkle the top with some of the breadcrumbs. Place in the oven and cook for 1½ hours, stirring every 20 minutes before sprinkling once more with breadcrumbs. Leave the last breadcrumb topping as a crust to break at the table when serving.

# LAPIN AUX PRUNEAUX D'AGEN

*Rabbit remains a staple ingredient in the south-west, where hunting game has been a way of life for many centuries. This recipe, with fat dark Agen prunes, relies on slow, gentle cooking to release the contrasting flavours.*

Preparation: 30 minutes, plus overnight
   marinating
Cooking: 2 hours

Serves 6

1.5kg rabbit joints
24 Agen prunes
500ml red wine
2 tbsp olive oil
150g lardons
24 button onions
2 sticks of celery, chopped
2 cloves of garlic, crushed, peeled and
   chopped
25g flour
2 sprigs of thyme
1 bay leaf
sea salt
freshly ground black pepper
75ml brandy or Armagnac

Place the rabbit and prunes in two separate dishes, cover each with the wine and leave to marinate overnight.

Heat the olive oil in a flameproof casserole dish, fry the lardons, then remove and place to one side. Take the rabbit pieces from the marinade and fry them gently until brown. Take them out of the casserole dish and put aside. Add the onions, fry them until brown, then take out and put aside. Add the celery and garlic and sauté gently for 5 minutes. Sprinkle in the flour, mixing to absorb the oil, then slowly add the wine from the rabbit and from the prunes, and blend to a smooth sauce. Return the lardons, rabbit and onions to the pot, along with the herbs and seasoning. Cover and simmer gently for 1 hour.

Stir in the prunes and brandy, then simmer for a further 40 minutes.

# PIGEON AU FLOC

*Most markets of the south-western region sell pigeons, which roast well and have a slightly gamey flavour (if you're having difficulty finding pigeon in England, ask for squab instead – it's another name for a young pigeon – from specialist butchers). This recipe combines the roast pigeon with the earthy taste of morels in season and a dash of floc – that utterly addictive Gascon mixture of fresh grape juice and Armagnac – for a sweet, luscious autumn dish.*

Preparation: 20 minutes
Cooking: 40 minutes

Serves 6

6 pigeons
sea salt
freshly ground black pepper
6 bay leaves
olive oil
150g butter
500g morels or other seasonal mushrooms,
    cleaned
2 cloves of garlic, crushed, peeled and
    diced
200ml red floc de Gascogne (or use port)
chives, to garnish (optional)

Heat the oven to 200°C/gas 6. Season the pigeons, place a bay leaf in each and put on a lightly oiled roasting tray. Use 100g of the butter to smear the pigeon breasts. Place in the oven and roast for 25 minutes, basting with the juices from time to time as they roast.

Heat the remaining butter in a frying pan and add the whole mushrooms. Cook for about 15 minutes over a medium heat, trying not to break the mushrooms when you stir them – they look beautiful if they retain their shape. In the last 3 minutes of cooking, add the garlic and fry gently. When the pigeons are cooked, remove them from the oven and keep warm. Drain the cooking juices into the mushroom pan, add the floc and increase the heat to reduce the liquid by half.

Serve the pigeons on a bed of mushrooms, topped with the sauce and garnished with chives, if you like.

## PERDRIX AUX PRUNEAUX

*Agen prunes have little in common with the small, miserable prunes we were forced to eat as children. These are plump, dark and heady, and work particularly well with the darker, sweeter meat of small birds like partridge and pigeon.*

Preparation: 30 minutes
Cooking: 1 hour

Serves 6

6 partridges, with giblets
25g butter
12 slices streaky bacon
sea salt
freshly ground black pepper

*For the stock:*
2 carrots, chopped
2 onions, chopped
1 bay leaf
1 sprig of thyme

*For the stuffing:*
2 cloves of garlic, crushed, peeled and
   chopped
2 medium potatoes, cooked and chopped
150g Agen prunes
100g walnuts, chopped
50g butter, melted

*To finish the sauce:*
25g plain flour
1 glass red wine
1 tbsp redcurrant jelly

Place the giblets in a pan. Add the stock ingredients, cover with water and simmer for 45 minutes under a lid.

Meanwhile, heat the oven to 190°C/gas 5. Put the stuffing ingredients in a bowl, season and mix well. Use the mixture to stuff the partridges, then rub them with the 25g butter and season. Lay 2 pieces of bacon on top of each bird, place in a roasting tin and cook for 15 minutes. Remove the bacon and keep warm, but cook the partridges for a further 15 minutes. Remove the cooked partridges from the oven and keep them warm for 15 minutes while you make the sauce.

Add the flour to the roasting pan and mix until smooth. Drain the giblet stock and gradually stir it into the roasting tin. Bring to the boil, then add the wine and redcurrant jelly and simmer for 4 minutes. Strain if necessary. Check the seasoning, and serve with the roasted stuffed partridges and bacon.

# CHEVREUIL AUX BAIES ROUGES

*Sweetness complements game very well, and rarely more so than with this intensely flavoured late-summer dish. The berry sauce is wonderfully sticky and tart, though not enough to overpower the venison's characteristic taste.*

Preparation: 20 minutes, plus overnight marinating
Cooking: 50 minutes

Serves 6

900g venison fillet
500ml red wine
2 cloves of garlic, crushed, peeled and chopped
4 juniper berries, crushed
1 tsp black peppercorns, crushed
1 bay leaf
2 tbsp olive oil
sea salt
freshly ground black pepper
1 tbsp vinegar
20g unrefined brown sugar
1 tsp arrowroot
200g fresh redcurrants or frozen mixed berries

Place the venison, red wine, garlic, juniper berries, peppercorns and bay leaf in a bowl and leave to marinate overnight.

Heat the oven to 180°C/gas 4. Remove the meat from the marinade and dry well with kitchen paper. Strain the marinade into a saucepan and simmer until it has reduced by half.

Heat the oil in a roasting pan directly on the hob and brown the meat all over on the outside, then place in the oven to roast – 30 minutes for rare, 40 minutes for medium, 45 minutes for well done.

Remove from the oven and allow to rest for 10 minutes. Pour off any cooking juices into the saucepan with the reduced marinade and season. Add the vinegar and brown sugar. Mix the arrowroot with a little water and add to the sauce. Stir until it thickens slightly, add the berries and cook on a low heat for 2 minutes. Carve the venison and serve with the berry sauce.

# CANARD À L'ORANGE

*This classic combination of crispy roast duck and tangy orange is difficult to beat at any time of year, but as a winter dish, with roast potatoes or honeyed parsnips, it is truly spectacular.*

Preparation: 30 minutes
Cooking: 1³/₄ hours

Serves 4–6

20g butter
2 carrots, chopped
2 onions, chopped
2 sticks of celery, chopped
2 bay leaves
2 sprigs of thyme
1 x 2.5kg duck, with giblets
sea salt
freshly ground black pepper
4 unwaxed oranges
1 unwaxed lemon
20g arrowroot
2 tbsp Grand Marnier
25g unrefined sugar
1 tbsp cider vinegar

Heat the oven to 200°C/gas 6. Grease a roasting tin with half of the butter. Add the chopped vegetables and herbs. Rub the duck with seasoning and place on top of the vegetables. Cover with foil and cook in the oven for 1 hour, then remove the foil and cook for a further 30 minutes, until the duck is golden.

While the duck is cooking, place the giblets in a small saucepan of water. Bring to the boil, then cover and simmer for 30 minutes.

Zest and juice 2 oranges and the lemon. Set aside the zest and juice. Cut the remaining oranges into wedges, then grease a roasting pan with the remaining butter and add the wedges. Roast in the oven for 20 minutes before serving.

When the duck is cooked, remove it from the roasting pan and keep it warm. Place the roasting pan directly on the hob and cook for 5 minutes to add extra colour to the vegetables. Carefully drain off the fat (reserve it for another use), without disturbing the sediment. Add about 400ml giblet stock, bring to the boil and simmer for 5 minutes. Remove from the heat, mix the arrowroot with a little water and add to the roasting pan. Stir well to thicken the sauce, then pass through a fine sieve into a saucepan. Add the Grand Marnier, sugar, vinegar, and the zest and juice you set aside earlier, and warm over a low heat, but do not allow to boil. Transfer the duck to a carving plate with the roasted orange wedges and serve with the sauce.

# MAGRET À L'ORANGE

*This is a summery version of the old classic, using chilli and fennel to spice up a sweet vegetable salad. Duck breasts should never be overcooked (I prefer mine to be just seared, so that the fat is crisp and sizzling); and in this case, the dish is best left to cool for a few minutes, to allow the flavours time to develop.*

Preparation: 30 minutes, plus an hour's marinating
Cooking: 20 minutes

Serves 6

3 duck breasts
zest and juice of 2 unwaxed oranges
2 hot chillies, diced
4 tbsp olive oil
1 head fennel
3 carrots
4 sticks of celery
2 red peppers
2 cloves of garlic
sea salt
freshly ground black pepper

Using a sharp knife, score the skin of each duck breast in a close criss-cross pattern. Put the orange zest and juice, chillies and half the oil in a bowl, add the duck breasts, coat them with the marinade, cover and leave for 1 hour.

Heat the remaining olive oil in a large frying pan. Take the duck from the marinade (keep the marinade) and put it into the pan, skin-side down. Fry for 5 minutes, then reduce the heat and continue to cook until golden (about 8 minutes). Turn the magrets over and cook for a further 6 minutes for rare, or 10 minutes for medium. Remove from the pan and leave to rest for 4 minutes. Pour the marinade into the pan and gently bring to a simmer, then remove from the heat and place on one side. Carve each breast into thin slices.

Trim and cut the fennel, carrots, celery and pepper into thin even-sized lengths. Crush, peel and chop the garlic. Add the vegetables and garlic to the warm marinade, season and toss well. Pile the salad onto serving plates and top with the sliced duck.

# CANARD AUX NAVETS

*This simple and time-honoured combination of duck breast, smoky-sweet shallots and fresh young turnips works very well as a warming winter dish.*

Preparation: 30 minutes
Cooking: 40 minutes

Serves 6

6 duck breasts
sea salt
freshly ground black pepper
1 tbsp goose or duck fat or olive oil
24 shallots
400g small turnips, cut into wedges
30g flour
400ml white wine
2 sprigs of thyme
2 bay leaves
1 tbsp brown sugar
100ml Madeira

Trim and season the duck breasts. Heat half the fat in a large pan, add the duck and cook over a moderate heat on each side until golden. Now reduce the heat and cook for a further 10 minutes. Peel the shallots: put them into a bowl with some boiling water for 2 minutes, then drain them and peel when cool. The skins should slip off easily.

In another large pan, heat the remaining fat. Add the shallots and turnips and cook until golden all over. Transfer the duck to this pan and continue to cook. In the first pan, make a roux: remove the pan from the heat, add the flour and mix well. Pour in the wine a little at a time and mix in. When all the wine is added, return to the heat and bring to the boil. Add the thyme, bay leaves and sugar. Pour over the duck and turnips and cook on a low heat for a further 8 minutes. Stir in the Madeira just before serving.

## RILLETTES DE CANARD

*This is absolutely the best way to use leftover duck, and it's still the most delicious sandwich filling I know…*

Preparation: 10 minutes
Cooking: 1½ hours

Serves 2

1 duck carcass, or 2 duck legs
200ml dry white wine
100ml water
sea salt
freshly ground black pepper
1 clove of garlic, crushed, peeled and
   chopped
1 pinch allspice
1 bay leaf
1 sprig of thyme

Cut the duck into manageable pieces and place in a saucepan. Add all the remaining ingredients, then cover with a tight-fitting lid and simmer gently for 1½ hours, stirring frequently. Check the liquid level and add a little more wine if needed. By this time the duck meat should have separated from the bones. Remove the bay leaf, thyme twig and bones from the meat. Spoon the remaining mixture into a small earthenware pot. Pour in any juices, then leave to cool and refrigerate. Serve with crusty bread and green salad.

## SALADE DE MAGRET

*Anyone visiting the markets and smallholdings of south-west France will have noticed the quantities of duck breeders selling smoked magrets de canard, dark, delicious, smoked breasts of duck sheathed in marbled fat. Bernard Mounet (wholeheartedly acknowledged as the 'Roi du Canard' throughout the region) gave us this ultra-simple recipe for a duck breast salad when we visited his farm. Serve it with floc, he advises, and good company. I see no reason to disagree.*

Preparation: 25 minutes

Serves 6

1 curly lettuce, washed
100g watercress
3 tbsp wine vinegar
1 tbsp Dijon mustard
6 tbsp olive oil
1 tbsp walnut oil
2 smoked duck breasts
sea salt
freshly ground black pepper
100g walnuts, chopped
a bunch of chervil, leaves finely chopped

Put the lettuce and watercress leaves into a large bowl. In a separate bowl, whisk together the vinegar and mustard, then slowly drizzle in the oils, continuously whisking. Slice the duck breasts as thinly as possible with a sharp knife. Add to the salad with the dressing, toss well, season and scatter over the walnuts and chervil. Serve at once with fresh bread.

# CONFIT DE CANARD

*Confit de canard is one of the principal ingredients of cassoulet (see page 158), although it makes an irresistible dish on its own. You can buy it from any market in the south-western region, but nothing beats the home-made version, which can be eaten warm and crispy straight away, or stored in the fridge for a deeper, more complex flavour.*

Preparation: 30 minutes, plus overnight
   steeping
Cooking: 2 hours

Serves 6

6 duck legs
4 tbsp sea salt
freshly ground black pepper
6 bay leaves
6 sprigs of thyme
1kg goose or duck fat

Rub the duck all over with the sea salt and black pepper. Place in a deep roasting dish with the herbs, cover and refrigerate overnight.

The following day, take the duck out of the dish and brush away the salt. Heat the oven to 150°C/gas 2. Return the duck to the cleaned dish, along with the fat, put in the oven and roast for 2 hours. Turn the duck halfway through cooking and baste occasionally. Sterilize a large Kilner jar by placing it in the hot oven for 5 minutes. When the duck is cooked, transfer it to the hot Kilner jar. Add the herbs, then strain the fat through a fine sieve into the jar until the meat is totally covered. Close the lid and leave to set.

This will keep for up to 2 months in the fridge. The confit will improve with age, although if you plan to eat the duck straight away, strain off the fat and store it in the fridge. (It makes terrific roast potatoes!)

# POULET CHASSEUR

*This traditional dish relies on the quality of its ingredients. Free-range chickens are the best, locally bred and fed on corn.*

Preparation: 30 minutes
Cooking: 45 minutes

Serves 6

50g butter
3 tbsp olive oil
2 small free-range chickens, each cut into
    6 pieces
3 shallots, chopped
2 cloves of garlic, crushed, peeled and
    chopped
300g brown mushrooms, cleaned and
    sliced
50g plain flour
200ml white wine
400ml chicken stock
1 tablespoon tomato purée
bunch of tarragon, chopped
bunch of flat-leaf parsley, chopped
bunch of chervil, chopped

Heat the butter and oil in a flameproof casserole and cook the chicken pieces (a few at a time) on each side until browned. Remove from the casserole and put aside. Add the shallots, garlic and sliced mushrooms to the pot and cook over a low heat for 8 minutes, then sprinkle in the flour and mix well so that it absorbs the oil. Slowly add a little wine, stirring constantly until blended. Repeat until all the wine and stock have been added, making a sauce. Then add the tomato purée, bring to the boil and reduce the heat. Return the chicken pieces to the pan and cover. Simmer for 30 minutes. Add the tarragon, parsley and chervil, mix through and serve.

# PÂTÉ DE FOIE

*The south-west of France is well-known for the variety and excellence of its terrines and pâtés, although few people realize how simple these can be to make at home. This chicken liver pâté is both quick and delicious to prepare, and can be adapted (with chestnuts, mushrooms, walnuts or any other seasonal ingredients) to suit any occasion. Serve with hot toast and salad.*

Preparation: 15 minutes
Cooking: 10 minutes, plus an hour's setting

Serves 6

600g chicken livers
150g unsalted butter
2 shallots, finely chopped
2 cloves of garlic, crushed, peeled and
    chopped
75ml red wine
sea salt
freshly ground black pepper
50ml double cream
generous sprig of thyme

Trim the chicken livers and cut into even-sized pieces. Heat half the butter in a pan and fry the livers for 3 minutes on a high heat, then remove from the pan and put aside. Reduce the heat, add the shallots and fry gently for 4 minutes, then add the garlic and fry for a further 2 minutes. Put the chicken livers, shallots and garlic into a food processor. Pour the red wine into the cooking pan and bring to the boil to deglaze the pan, then add to the processor along with the seasoning and cream. Blend until smooth. Transfer to a sterile Kilner jar or serving bowl and smooth over the top. Place the remaining butter and the thyme in a small pan and melt the butter, then pick out the thyme and place it on top of the pâté. Pour the butter over the pâté, then place in the fridge to cool and set for at least 1 hour.

## POULET À LA MOUTARDE DE DIJON

*This is an absurdly quick and easy-to-make dish that works especially well as a light summer meal. Serve with fresh watercress tossed in vinaigrette.*

Preparation: 20 minutes, plus at least an hour's
    marinating
Cooking: 25 minutes

Serves 6

6 tbsp Dijon mustard
zest and juice of 2 unwaxed lemons
3 cloves of garlic, crushed, peeled and
    chopped
2 tsp paprika
6 chicken breasts
olive oil, for the baking sheet

Mix together the mustard, lemon zest and juice, garlic and paprika, and coat the chicken generously with the mixture. Leave to marinate for at least 1 hour.

    Heat the oven to 180°C/gas 4. Lightly oil a baking sheet, put the chicken breasts on it – with the marinade smeared over them – and roast for 25 minutes.

## TERRINE DE CAMPAGNE

*This meat terrine is traditionally made in an earthenware terrine dish, which ensures that it cooks evenly, but you can use a loaf tin instead. Serve it sliced, with crusty bread and a fresh green salad. Pistachios work well in this terrine, giving it a slightly sweet flavour and a crunchy texture: add about 100g chopped nuts to the final mixture and garnish with a few whole nuts on top.*

Preparation: 30 minutes,
    plus 2 hours' cooling and pressing
Cooking: 1½ hours

Serves 6

200g chicken livers, trimmed
450g streaky bacon, thinly sliced
500g lean pork, diced
200g minced pork
4 shallots, finely diced
2 eggs, beaten
bunch of fresh flat-leaf parsley, chopped
4 sprigs of thyme, leaves pulled off
2 bay leaves, chopped
sea salt
freshly ground black pepper

Heat the oven to 160°C/gas 3. Chop the chicken livers and 250g of the streaky bacon and place in a bowl. Add the chopped and the minced pork, the shallots, eggs, herbs and seasoning, and mix well. Line a 22cm by 11cm terrine dish or loaf tin with most of the remaining bacon slices, reserving some for the top. Fill the dish with the meat mixture and pat down until smooth. Fold over the protruding bacon and lay the remaining slices on top. Bake in the oven for 1½ hours. Remove and leave to cool for 30 minutes and then carefully drain off the juice (you can keep this for another meat recipe). Place a weight over the terrine that fits snugly on top to compress it for 1½ hours.

Turn out the terrine (if you prefer) while it is still just warm. Refrigerate, slice and serve. This terrine will keep for up to 7 days in the fridge.

# Desserts

The first impact is always visual. The shapes, colours and designs of the French pâtisserie take the concept of dessert far beyond mere appetite and into performance art. The jewelled cakes are lifted carefully into their presentation boxes, decorated with paper flowers and long curls of multicoloured ribbon. This takes time; it demands reverence. There is an unspoken etiquette both in the buying and in the eating of these little pieces of whimsy, a general understanding of the work that has gone into their creation. Still, for me the real delight is the atmosphere of the place: the mingled scents of caramel, of fruits preserved in Armagnac, of chocolate, mocha, vanilla and freshly baked croissants. And the anticipation of flavours – fresh fruits on *pâte brisée* and *crème anglaise*; bitter chocolate sprinkled over the bright-green icing of a *Salammbô*; a fat baba soaking regally in sugar and dark rum…

French tradition uses desserts sparingly, but to effect. Most families will usually end a meal with cheese, fruit or yoghurt during the week, but at weekends, the celebratory dessert comes into its own. Every village has its pâtisserie, and on Sunday mornings the shop window will be artfully crammed with cakes, tarts and *pièces montées* – those elegant mountains of choux buns mortared together with caramel and chocolate.

It would be futile to try to duplicate the spectacular work of those master pâtissiers. However, there are plenty more ways to explore and enjoy those luscious ingredients. This section provides a few ideas on how to adapt and re-create at home some of France's best-loved desserts and pastries.

# CRÈME CARAMEL

*This silken, unctuous dish belongs to the large family of crèmes renversées – cream-based dishes cooked in a bain-marie and served upside-down – and this version remains one of the best known and best loved of French desserts. Dumas suggests a variety of alternative flavours – rosewater, pistachio, lemon, coffee – but in all cases the basic technique remains the same.*

Preparation: 25 minutes
Cooking: 45 minutes

Serves 6

*For the caramel:*
150g unrefined caster sugar

*For the cream:*
650ml milk
4 eggs
100g unrefined caster sugar
1 vanilla pod

Place the caster sugar for the caramel in a small heavy-based pan and warm over a gentle heat, allowing it to melt. Once the sugar has melted, increase the heat a little to get a good caramel colour, then pour either into individual ovenproof dishes or into one large dish, coating the bottom completely. Leave to cool.

Heat the oven to 150°C/gas 2. Heat the milk to a shivering simmer. Beat the eggs and sugar together in a bowl, then add the hot milk and mix well. Cut the vanilla pod in half lengthways, scrape out the seeds and add them to the milk. Pour the mixture into the prepared dishes (if using individual pots, make sure to give the mixture a stir each time to distribute the vanilla seeds evenly). Place the dishes in a deep roasting pan and almost fill with hot water from the kettle. Place in the oven and cook for 45 minutes until set to the touch.

Remove and allow to cool, then turn out. Spoon any remaining caramel from the pots over the puddings, and serve.

## BAVAROISE AU CAFÉ

*There are any number of variants on the classic bavaroise. I particularly love chocolate and blackcurrant versions – for these, substitute the coffee in this recipe for either cocoa powder or crème de cassis.*

Preparation: 45 minutes, plus 2 hours' setting
Cooking: 5 minutes

Serves 6

400ml milk
3 tbsp ground coffee
60g unrefined sugar
4 egg yolks
4 leaves gelatine or 4 tsp powdered
225ml double cream, plus extra to serve
50g dark chocolate

Heat the milk almost to boiling point, add the coffee, mix well and allow to sit for 5 minutes. Place the sugar and egg yolks in a bowl and whisk until light and fluffy, then pass the warm coffee through a fine sieve (to remove the grounds) into the bowl and stir it in. Pour back into the pan, return to a low heat and cook, stirring constantly with a wooden spoon, until the mixture thickens and coats the back of the spoon – do not overheat! Soak the gelatine, following the instructions on the packet, add to the coffee mixture and stir well. Transfer to a bowl and allow to cool.

Whisk the cream until it just holds its shape, then fold into the coffee mixture. Pour into one large serving dish or individual glasses. Place in the fridge to set. Garnish with a little extra whipped cream and chocolate curls (use a potato peeler or sharp knife).

## SEMOULE AU CITRON

*This Moorish dish may have come to France as far back as the Crusades. Combining polenta for its rich, dense texture and lemon for its sharp, sweet taste, it's excellent served on its own, or with vanilla ice cream or a simple coulis of red summer fruits.*

Preparation: 15 minutes
Cooking: 25 minutes

Serves 4–6

100g butter
50ml milk
1 vanilla pod
100g polenta
50g self-raising flour
100g icing sugar
3 large eggs
zest and juice of 1 unwaxed lemon
2 tbsp Armagnac

Heat the oven to 180°C/gas 4. Grease an ovenproof dish with a little of the butter. Warm the remaining butter and the milk in a saucepan. Cut the vanilla pod in half and scrape the seeds out of the pod into the milk. Place the polenta, flour and icing sugar in a mixing bowl. Mix together and make a well in the centre.

Crack the eggs into a bowl and whisk. Stir in the warm milk, then pour into the polenta and flour mixture. Mix until smooth. Add the lemon zest, juice and Armagnac. Stir well and pour into the greased dish. Bake in the oven for 25 minutes.

## BRIOCHE PERDUE

*There are a number of French recipes designed to use up stale bread. This elegant version of bread-and-butter pudding works very well with fresh or stale brioche – although, let's be honest, does anyone ever let brioche go stale? – and the addition of the floc (see page 165) gives a grown-up sophistication to a comfort-food favourite.*

Preparation: 15 minutes, plus at least an
   hour's soaking
Cooking: 45 minutes

Serves 6

75g soft butter
6 slices of brioche, about 275g altogether
3–4 apples
100g plump raisins
100ml white floc (or a sweet white wine)
3 eggs
300ml milk
60g unrefined soft brown sugar

Grease an ovenproof dish and spread the brioche with the butter. Peel and core the apples and slice. Scatter the apples and raisins over the bottom of the dish, then arrange the brioche in overlapping layers over the top. Whisk together the floc, eggs and milk, and pour over the brioche, making sure that all the slices are coated. Using a palette knife, push the brioche down to enable the egg mixture to soak in. Sprinkle the sugar over the top and place in the fridge for at least an hour (or overnight).

   Heat the oven to 150°C/gas 2. Bake the pudding for 45 minutes, until the mixture has set and the pudding has a golden top.

## PÊCHES AU CARDINAL

*Quite a number of classic French desserts seem to come to us via various members of the clergy. I'm not sure who the original cardinal was (though I like to think it was Richelieu, the arch-enemy of Dumas' Three Musketeers), but this has got to be one of the most delicious ways of serving fresh peaches. Fran advises sieving and blitzing the raspberries, while I prefer the coulis to be rather more as Nature intended. If you're feeling truly irredeemable, try substituting a tablespoon of raspberry or blackcurrant liqueur for the water…*

Preparation: 30 minutes
Cooking: 5 minutes

Serves 6

6 ripe peaches
300g raspberries
200g icing sugar
1 tbsp water
60g toasted almonds

Either peel the peaches (plunge them into a saucepan of boiling water for 40 seconds, allow to cool for a few minutes, then remove the skin) or simply wash and dry them. Put them on a serving plate.

Put the raspberries, icing sugar and water in a blender and blitz to a purée. Pass through a sieve to remove all the seeds. Pour the raspberry coulis over the peaches, and sprinkle with toasted almonds.

## PETITS POTS AU CITRON

*These colourful little lemon berry pots are the ideal dessert for summer, combining fresh seasonal berries with tangy lemon cream. Lovely with finger biscuits and crème fraîche.*

Preparation: 5 minutes, plus cooling time
Cooking: 30 minutes

Serves 6

400g blueberries or other soft fruit in
    season
zest and juice of 3 unwaxed lemons
150g unrefined caster sugar
4 eggs
300ml double cream
75g icing sugar

Heat the oven to 150°C/gas 2. Divide the berries between 6 ramekins. If using fruit such as apricots or peaches, halve them, remove the stone, then chop the fruit and place in the ramekins.

Put the lemon zest and juice, sugar and eggs into a large bowl and whisk until smooth, then stir in the cream. Pour the lemon cream into the 6 ramekins and put the ramekins in a deep roasting dish. Make a bain-marie by half filling the dish with hot water. Bake for 30 minutes. Remove and allow to cool.

When cold, dust with icing sugar and place under a hot grill until the icing sugar caramelizes and turns golden. Cool again before serving.

# TARTE AUX CERISES

*I think the cherry makes the most beautiful of fresh-fruit tarts, although of course you can use whatever fruit appeals to you according to the season. For me, though, the cherry is the perfect fruit, and there are so many different species to choose from at various times of year: the fat black morello cherry, the bright-red cherries of early summer, the musky-flavoured yellow ones of autumn or the sour-sweet griottes that make such excellent liqueur.*

Preparation: 1 hour, plus an hour's chilling
Cooking: 30 minutes

Serves 6

For the pâte sablée:
240g plain flour
160g butter, plus extra for greasing
100g icing sugar, plus extra for dusting
2 egg yolks

For the topping:
2 tbsp redcurrant jelly
200ml cream
200g crème fraîche
2 tbsp kirsch
700g cherries
1 tbsp icing sugar

To make the pastry, sift the flour into a large bowl, add the butter and rub together with your fingertips until it resembles breadcrumbs. Add the icing sugar and mix through. Whisk the egg yolks, add to the mixture and combine using a round-bladed knife in a cutting motion to form a pastry ball. Wrap in cling film and chill in the fridge for 30 minutes. Lightly grease a 25cm flan ring and baking sheet or 6 individual tart tins with butter, and lightly dust a cool surface with icing sugar. Roll out the pastry and line the tin or tins. Return to the fridge and chill for 30 minutes.

Heat the oven to 180°C/gas 4. Line the pastry case or cases with baking paper and cooking beans, place in the oven and bake for 10 minutes. Carefully remove the baking paper and beans, return to the oven and bake for a further 15 minutes or until golden. Remove and leave to cool.

Melt the redcurrant jelly and brush a layer over the bottom of the pastry case. Whip the cream to soft folds, add the crème fraîche and whisk until blended. Then stir in the kirsch. Pile the cream in the pastry case or cases, top with cherries and dust with icing sugar.

# ÎLES FLOTTANTES

*These 'floating islands' have been popular for hundreds of years, and make a spectacular, and only slightly fiddly dessert to prepare. Don't stress too much over the meringues; if the traditional method seems daunting, then cook them in the oven instead at 110°C/gas ½ for 5–8 minutes. It's just as good and will remove any anxiety at the cooker!*

Preparation: 30 minutes
Cooking: 30 minutes

Serves 6

*For the custard:*
600ml milk
100g unrefined sugar
1 vanilla pod
5 egg yolks

*For the meringues:*
3 egg whites
90g unrefined caster sugar

*To finish:*
toasted flaked almonds
75g unrefined sugar

To make the custard, warm the milk and sugar in a saucepan. Cut the vanilla pod in half, scrape out the seeds and stir them into the milk. Whisk the egg yolks in a bowl, and when the milk is almost boiling, pour it into the egg yolks and whisk. Fill a pan big enough to hold the bowl with hot water to a depth of 5cm. Whisk the custard frequently in this bain-marie over a low heat until it thickens (this will take about 10 minutes). When the custard is made, pour it into one large serving dish or 6 individual ones, then cover the custard with cling film – touching the surface – to avoid a skin forming. Place to one side.

For the meringue, half fill a wide low-sided pan with water and bring to a gentle simmer. Using an electric whisk, beat the egg whites until stiff, then add the sugar and whisk in until smooth and shiny. Shape the mixture into 'islands', using two dessertspoons, and place in the simmering water. Cook in batches of 3 or 4 at a time, for 30 seconds on one side, then turn and cook for a further 30 seconds on the other. Remove with a slotted spoon and place on a clean kitchen cloth to remove excess water. Repeat until all the meringue mixture is used – this should make 12 islands.

Take the cling film off the custard. Place the meringue islands on the custard and sprinkle with the flaked almonds. Put the sugar into a small non-stick pan and cook over a gentle heat until dissolved and just turned golden-caramel, then drizzle over the meringues.

Traditionally this dish is served cold, but it is also rather delicious warm.

# TARTE BELLE HÉLÈNE

*Pears and chocolate have always been something of a winning combination. Use firm, ripe yellow pears for this recipe, and serve just warm with vanilla ice cream and curls of dark chocolate. The pastry is a delicate, crumbly sweet one, used only for desserts.*

Preparation: 1 hour, plus an hour's chilling
Cooking: 45 minutes

Serves 6

*For the pâte sucrée:*
60g butter, plus extra for greasing
140g plain flour
50g icing sugar, plus extra for dusting
1–2 medium egg yolks

*For the filling:*
3 ripe pears
75g butter
75g unrefined sugar
1 egg
20g ground almonds
75g self-raising flour
¼ tsp baking powder
25g cocoa
50ml milk

Heat the oven to 190°C/gas 5. Lightly butter a 25cm flan ring and place it on a buttered baking sheet.

To make the pastry, sift the flour into a large bowl, add the butter and rub together with your fingertips until the texture resembles breadcrumbs. Now add the icing sugar and mix through. Whisk the egg yolks, add to the mixture and combine, using a round-bladed knife in a cutting motion until it forms a pastry ball. Wrap in cling film and chill in the fridge for 30 minutes. Lightly dust a cool surface with icing sugar, roll the pastry out to fit just inside the flan ring, then carefully drape the pastry over the rolling pin and unroll it into the flan ring on the baking sheet. Using your fingers, mould the pastry into the ring to form the base of the tart, then chill for a further 30 minutes.

For the filling, peel, core and halve the pears and arrange round-side up in the pastry case. Cream together the butter and sugar. Add the egg and beat in, then mix in the ground almonds. Sift the flour, baking powder and cocoa, and fold in with the milk. Spoon into the pastry case and smooth the top. Place in the oven and bake for 30 minutes, then cover with tin foil and bake for a further 15 minutes. Dust with a little icing sugar before serving.

## COMPOTE DE POMMES AUX PRUNEAUX D'AGEN

*Most families have a version of this recipe, which makes the most of any fruit in season. Here the prunes and spices give an almost mulled taste to the autumn apples, which can be eaten on their own or chilled and topped with chantilly and chocolate curls for a more festive look. Fran suggests this as an excellent accompaniment to home-made muesli (just mix some assorted dried fruits, seeds, nuts and rolled oats with a spoonful of maple syrup and toast in the oven until brown), while I like to substitute 400ml plum liqueur for the water as a warming, wintry treat.*

Preparation: 20 minutes
Cooking: 30 minutes

Serves 6

600g Agen prunes, or fresh plums, halved
   and pitted
8 apples, peeled, cored and cut into wedges
150g unrefined soft brown sugar
2 tsp mixed spice
400ml water

Heat the oven to 180°C/gas 4. Put the prepared fruit in an ovenproof dish, sprinkle with the sugar and spice and add the water, then cover and place in the oven for 1 hour. Remove and leave to cool. This compote gets better and richer with time, so if possible make it the day before and store it in the fridge.

# CROISSANTS

*Croissants are the essential French pastry. Fresh baked for breakfast or smothered in almonds for the goûter, there's something wonderful about the flaky, almost brittle crust and the soft, fragrant centre of these simple little pastries. Of course you can buy croissants (or what purport to be croissants) ready-made from supermarkets everywhere but, believe me, nothing – nothing – beats the real deal, baked to perfection in your own oven and eaten hot, with a cup of bitter chocolate.*

Preparation: 3 hours including proving time
Cooking: 12–15 minutes

Makes 12–14

500g plain, or strong plain, flour, plus
   extra for dusting
45g unrefined sugar
1 tsp salt
15g fresh yeast, available from bakeries
200ml lukewarm water
100ml lukewarm milk
250g butter, plus extra for greasing
1 egg

*Note* You can make the pastry the night before to have early-morning fresh croissants! And see overleaf for a visual guide to the method.

Sift the flour, sugar and salt into a large bowl. Crumble the yeast into the warm water and milk, mix and leave for 5 minutes to dissolve. Make a well in the middle of the flour and pour in the yeast mixture. Stir in the liquid, gradually drawing in the flour, until you have a smooth dough. Shape into a ball, cover and leave to rest in the fridge for 20 minutes.

Place the butter between two sheets of greaseproof paper and beat it with a rolling pin until flat and about 20cm square. Dust a surface with flour and roll the dough out to a

40cm square, place the flattened butter in the middle and fold the dough over as if wrapping a parcel. Roll the dough out to a rectangle 24cm by 60cm. Dust with a little extra flour so that the dough does not stick to the work surface, if needed. Fold one third of the dough on top of the other and then fold over the remaining third. Turn 90 degrees, roll out again, then fold again as described above. Wrap in cling film and place in the fridge to rest for 30 minutes. Repeat the rolling out and folding two more times, then wrap the dough in cling film and return to the fridge to relax for a further 30 minutes.

Make a triangular template measuring 21cm by 21cm by 14cm. Lightly butter a baking sheet.

Roll out the dough to 42cm by 42cm. Cut the dough in half horizontally, then mark out the triangles with the template and cut them out. Roll the dough from the base of each triangle, then shape into a crescent and place on the baking sheet with the point underneath so that the croissant will not unravel. Cover and leave to rise in a warm draught-free room until the croissants have doubled in size. (This could be done overnight.)

Heat the oven to 220°C/gas 7. Whisk the egg and brush each croissant, then bake them in the oven for 15 minutes.

*For almond croissants* Follow the instructions as above, and as soon as you remove the croissants from the oven, cut them in half horizontally and spread with almond paste. Sandwich together, spread a little almond paste on top, and sprinkle with toasted almonds and a dusting of icing sugar. (You can buy almond paste from a delicatessen, or make it yourself by blitzing 100g almonds, 150g unrefined caster sugar and a small knob of butter in a food processor.)

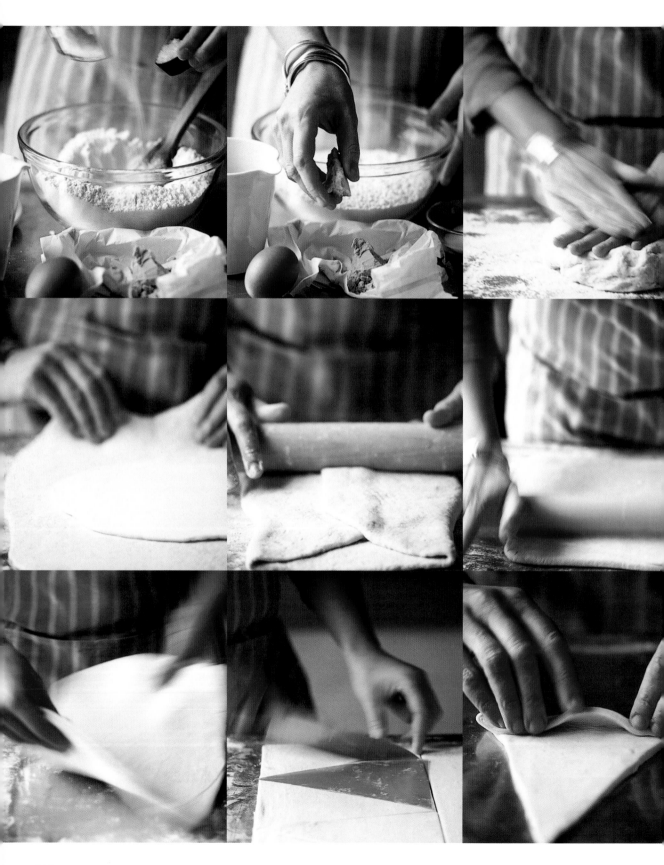

# CHICHIS

*These frivolous little sugared pastries are available fresh on most typical markets of the south-west, and the smell of them cooking is intoxicating. Eat them hot and dusted with icing sugar or with a generous splash of maple syrup.*

Preparation: 30 minutes, plus an hour's proving
Cooking: 10 minutes

Serves 4

7g fresh yeast
45g unrefined sugar
175ml warm milk
230g plain flour
2 egg yolks, beaten
vegetable oil, for deep frying
unrefined caster sugar, for dusting

Dissolve the yeast and sugar in the warm milk. Sift the flour into a bowl and make a well in the centre. Mix the egg yolks with the yeast and milk, and pour into the flour. Combine to a smooth soft dough, then knead for 10 minutes. Grease the inside of a large bowl. Place the dough in it, cover and leave to prove in a warm place for an hour. It will double in size. Lightly knead the dough on a floured surface and then roll into 5cm-long sausages. Leave to rest for 10 minutes before cooking.

Heat the oil in a deep-fat fryer or large saucepan. To test if it is hot enough, add a cube of bread: it should brown within 1 minute. Add a few dough sausages at a time. They will sink and resurface. Turn them when golden underneath, and when golden all over, remove them with a slotted spoon, drain and roll generously in caster sugar.

# GÂTEAU BASQUE

*This delicious, moist cake originates from the Basque region, where almonds are plentiful and are used in many types of pastry.*

Preparation: 1 hour
Cooking: 45 minutes

Serves 6

*For the pâte à l'amande:*
225g butter, plus extra for greasing
300g plain flour
50g ground almonds
150g icing sugar, plus extra for dusting
zest of 1 unwaxed lemon
3–4 egg yolks, beaten

*For the filling:*
400ml milk
1 vanilla pod
6 egg yolks
200g unrefined sugar
25g flour
30g ground almonds
150g jam
1 egg yolk, beaten
icing sugar, for dusting

Butter a 25cm high-sided flan ring and baking sheet.

Sift the flour into a large bowl, add the butter and rub together with your fingertips until it resembles breadcrumbs. Add the ground almonds, icing sugar and lemon zest, and mix in thoroughly. Whisk the egg yolks, add and mix in with a round-bladed knife using a cutting motion until it all comes together to form a pastry ball. Wrap in cling film and chill in the fridge for 30 minutes. Dust a cool surface with icing sugar, roll out three-quarters of the pastry to at least 5cm larger than the flan ring, then carefully roll the pastry on to the rolling pin and drape over the flan ring on the baking sheet. Mould the pastry into the ring, trim off any excess with a knife and chill for a further 30 minutes. Roll out the remaining pastry to fit the top of the flan ring, cover and place in the fridge to chill.

Warm the milk in a saucepan. Split the vanilla pod in half, scrape out the seeds and add them to the milk. Mix the egg yolks and sugar in a bowl, then stir in the flour and almonds. Pour in the hot milk, stirring all the time. Return the mixture to the pan and place over a low heat, stirring constantly until it thickens. Remove from the heat and leave to cool, and it will thicken some more.

Heat the oven to 180°C/gas 4. Spread the jam over the base of the pastry, add the cool custard and smooth over the top. Brush the edges of the pastry with egg and place the lid on top. Trim the edges and crimp together. Score the surface of the pastry with a knife in a criss-cross pattern, brush with egg and bake for 45 minutes. Check that the top does not brown too much – cover with tin foil if necessary. Leave to cool for at least 30 minutes, and dust with icing sugar before serving.

## PAIN AUX NOIX

*This sweet nut loaf, made with soft fresh walnuts, is the perfect accompaniment to cheese and fruit.*

Preparation: 20 minutes
Cooking: 1 hour 5 minutes

Serves 6

200g walnuts
200g butter
100g unrefined soft brown sugar
100g honey
2 eggs, beaten
300ml milk
350g self-raising flour
1 tsp baking powder
1 tbsp icing sugar

Heat the oven to 180°C/gas 4. Line a 25cm by 12cm loaf tin with baking paper. Blitz the walnuts in a food processor until finely chopped.

Melt the butter, sugar and honey in a medium pan over a gentle heat. When melted and blended, remove from the heat and stir in the walnuts. Whisk together the eggs and milk and add to the walnut mix, then add the flour and baking powder and blend until smooth. Pour into the prepared loaf tin and bake for 30 minutes, then reduce the heat to 150°C/gas 2 and bake for a further 30 minutes. Cool for 10 minutes, remove from the tin and dust with icing sugar. Best eaten at least 24 hours later – just wrap in tin foil when cool.

# Special Dedication

In 2003, I decided to donate my part of the proceeds from *The French Kitchen* to Médecins Sans Frontières, an organization I have supported for many years which provides essential medical aid for some of the poorest and most troubled countries in the world.

That year I went with MSF to the Congo to see for myself how the money was being used to combat sleeping sickness, a fatal disease if left untreated, which kills up to half a million people a year. We travelled up the Congo by canoe and riverboat, screening and treating whole villages for the disease. Without treatment, every person who tested positive would have died.

In a society where the idea of miracles has become irrelevant and outdated, it's hard to imagine the true impact of this. In a society where it is considered almost normal for African children to die of easily curable diseases, it is hard to imagine that one small cookbook – or even two – can make much of a difference.

Believe me, it can.

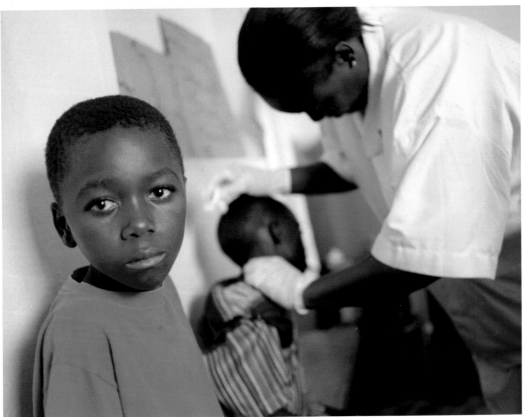

Photo by Tom Craig

This is Boniface. He is eight years old, and he owes you his life.

*All Joanne Harris's proceeds from* The French Market *will go to MSF in order to help them continue their work in the Congo.*

# Index

# List of Recipes

fruits de mer à l'aïoli (seafood platter with garlic mayonnaise), 114

garbure (bean and cabbage soup with Roquefort cheese), 28
gâteau Basque (rich almond cake), 223
gougère au jambon (choux pastry puffs with ham filling), 31

haricots en salade (broad bean salad with soft goat's cheese), 73
haricots variés à la ciboulette (spring vegetables with fresh herbs), 83
huîtres aux lardons (grilled oysters with bacon), 117

îles flottantes (floating islands), 206

lapin aux pruneaux d'Agen (rabbit with red wine and prunes), 162
légumes rôtis sur petits toasts (roast vegetables on sourdough toast), 99
lentilles du Puy (Puy lentils in red wine and herbs), 103
lentilles en salade (tomato and lentil salad), 73
lotte aux girolles (monkfish with cream and girolle mushrooms), 138

magret à l'orange (warm duck salad with chilli and orange), 173
maquereau à la Dijonnaise (mackerel with leeks and Dijon mustard), 124
mayonnaise, 52
melon au floc (melon with floc), 60
mullet au poivron rouge (red mullet with chillies and peppers), 126

navets au vin blanc (baby turnips in white wine), 91

pain aux noix (sweet walnut loaf), 224
pâté de foie (chicken liver pâté), 182
pêches au cardinal (chilled peaches with raspberries), 200
perdrix aux pruneaux (partridge with prunes), 166
petites courgettes farcies (stuffed baby courgettes), 89
petits pots au citron (lemon berry pots), 203
pigeon au floc (pigeon with floc), 165
poireaux au poivron rouge (red peppers in balsamic vinegar), 99
poivrons farcis (stuffed red peppers), 90
pommes à l'Auvergnate (garlic mash with Cantal cheese), 79
pommes de terre aux cèpes (potatoes with cèpe mushrooms), 80
pommes de terre aux herbes (potatoes with garlic and herbs), 79
pommes de terre aux truffes (potatoes with truffles), 80
pommes de terre en salade (potato salad with tomatoes and herbs), 66
porc aux cèpes (pork with cèpe mushrooms), 156
porc aux châtaignes (pork with chestnuts), 155
porc aux pruneaux (pork with apple and prunes), 155

potage bonne femme (leek and potato soup), 23

poulet à la moutarde de Dijon (roast chicken with Dijon mustard), 184

poulet chasseur (chicken, wine and mushroom casserole), 181

rillettes de canard (shredded duck pâté), 177

rouille (garlic and chilli mayonnaise sauce), 55

Saint-Jacques aux pommes vapeur (king scallops with bacon and tarragon potatoes), 136

salade aux noix (walnut salad), 66

salade d'automne (apple and walnut salad), 76

salade de calamars (warm squid salad), 121

salade de concombre (cucumber salad), 59

salade de crabe à l'avocat (crab and avocado salad), 121

salade de magret (smoked duck salad), 177

salade de marmande (Marmande tomato salad), 59

salade des champs de mer (melon dill and prawn salad), 60

salade printanière (spring salad with boiled eggs, lettuce and smoked bacon), 65

salade tiède au Camembert (warm camembert salad), 70

salade Toulousaine (warm salad of chickpeas and haricot beans with Toulouse sausages), 70

sauce aux noix (rich walnut dressing), 56

saumon au champagne (salmon in champagne), 126

seiche farcie (squid stuffed with garlic and pork), 118

semoule au citron (lemon polenta cake), 198

sole vapeur (steamed sole with chervil and lemon dressing), 122

soufflé au Roquefort (Roquefort cheese soufflé), 43

soupe au chou-fleur (cauliflower and Brie soup), 18

soupe aux haricots (cannellini bean and tomato soup), 22

soupe aux moules (creamy mussel soup with saffron), 21

soupe du vigneron (mushroom soup with red wine), 25

soupe printanière (broad bean soup), 18

tarte au chèvre (goat's cheese tart), 38

tarte aux cerises (fresh cherry tart with kirsch), 205

tarte Belle Hélène (pear and chocolate flan), 209

tartelettes aux champignons des bois (wild mushroom tartlets), 34

terrine de campagne (country pork and chicken terrine), 186

thon aux deux haricots (two-bean tuna), 134

tourte au Camembert (vegetable flan with camembert topping), 104

truite à l'étouffée (baked trout with leeks and potatoes), 133

truite de mer sauce verte (grilled sea bream in a herb and caper sauce), 130

turbot aux crevettes roses (turbot with prawns), 132

vinaigrette aux herbes (vinaigrette dressing with herbs), 56

# CONVERSION TABLES

| Weights | |
|---|---|
| 5g | $\frac{1}{4}$oz |
| 15g | $\frac{1}{2}$oz |
| 20g | $\frac{3}{4}$oz |
| 25g | 1oz |
| 50g | 2oz |
| 75g | 3oz |
| 125g | 4oz |
| 150g | 5oz |
| 175g | 6oz |
| 200g | 7oz |
| 250g | 8oz |
| 275g | 9oz |
| 300g | 10oz |
| 325g | 11oz |
| 375g | 12oz |
| 400g | 13oz |
| 425g | 14oz |
| 475g | 15oz |
| 500g | 1lb |
| 625g | $1\frac{1}{4}$ lb |
| 750g | $1\frac{1}{2}$ lb |
| 875g | $1\frac{3}{4}$ lb |
| 1kg | 2lb |
| 1.25g | $2\frac{1}{2}$ lb |
| 1.5kg | 3lb |
| 1.75kg | $3\frac{1}{2}$ lb |
| 2kg | 4lb |

| Liquids | |
|---|---|
| 15ml | $\frac{1}{2}$fl oz |
| 25ml | 1fl oz |
| 50ml | 2fl oz |
| 75ml | 3fl oz |
| 100ml | $3\frac{1}{2}$fl oz |
| 125ml | 4fl oz |
| 150ml | $\frac{1}{4}$ pint |
| 175ml | 6fl oz |
| 200ml | 7fl oz |
| 250ml | 8fl oz |
| 275ml | 9fl oz |
| 300ml | $\frac{1}{2}$ pint |
| 325ml | 11fl oz |
| 350ml | 12fl oz |
| 375ml | 13fl oz |
| 400ml | 14fl oz |
| 450ml | $\frac{3}{4}$ pint |
| 475ml | 16fl oz |
| 500ml | 17fl oz |
| 550ml | 18fl oz |
| 600ml | 1 pint |
| 750ml | $1\frac{1}{4}$ pints |
| 900ml | $1\frac{1}{2}$ pints |
| 1 litre | $1\frac{3}{4}$ pints |
| 1.2 litres | 2 pints |
| 1.5 litres | $2\frac{1}{2}$ pints |
| 1.8 litres | 3 pints |

| Oven temperatures | | |
|---|---|---|
| 110°C | 225°F | gas $\frac{1}{4}$ |
| 120°C | 250°F | gas $\frac{1}{2}$ |
| 140°C | 275°F | gas 1 |
| 150°C | 300°F | gas 2 |
| 160°C | 325°F | gas 3 |
| 180°C | 350°F | gas 4 |
| 190°C | 375°F | gas 5 |
| 200°C | 400°F | gas 6 |
| 220°C | 425°F | gas 7 |
| 230°C | 450°F | gas 8 |
| 240°C | 475°F | gas 9 |

# ACKNOWLEDGEMENTS

Heartfelt thanks to everyone who helped in the production of this book, especially to:

Madame Labadie, for sharing her family recipes

M. and Mme Sarrauste at the chocolaterie, La Cigale

M. Mounet, the Roi du Canard

M. Tadieu, for his award-winning floc

The Baron family, who showed us the largest and tastiest radishes we have ever eaten

Terrance and Angela Stokes, for letting us photograph their wonderful home

Sue and Mike, for their lovely gîte and wealth of local information

Anne-Laure at Laurent Perrier

Caroline at Moët & Chandon

Mark Housden, for lovely props from The French House

Eurostar for a speedy journey to Paris: www.eurostar.co.uk

Serafina Clarke

Stephanie Cabot

Francesca Liversidge

Debi Treloar

Mari Roberts

Fiona Andreanelli

Stuart Haygarth

Helen Trent

Anna Burgess-Lumsden, for assisting in the kitchen

Finally, to all the stallholders at markets in France who so kindly welcomed us, and the local shops back in England who worked hard to find produce to match for photography: Andreas Georghiou fine fruit and vegetables, Mortimer and Bennet deli, Covent Garden fishmongers, Macken Brothers butchers and Fishworks – all on Turnham Green Terrace, London W4.

Thank you to all of you. We could never have done it alone.